GREAT EXPECTATIONS

Your Family's Roadmap to
Guaranteed SAT/ACT Success

Chris Ajemian

GREAT EXPECTATIONS:
YOUR FAMILY'S ROADMAP TO GUARANTEED SAT/ACT SUCCESS

Copyright © 2018 Chris Ajemian
All rights reserved
First edition
ISBN 978-1-7328181-2-5

Published by:
CATES LLC
205 E 42nd St, 16th Floor
New York, NY 10017
United States

catestutoring.com

No part of this publication may be reproduced, stored in a retrieval system, or transmitted in any form or by any means, electronic, mechanical, photocopying, recording, or otherwise, without the prior written permission of the copyright owner.

This book is sold subject to the condition that it shall not, by way of trade or otherwise, be lent, resold, hired out, or otherwise circulated without the publisher's prior consent in any form of binding or cover other than that in which it is published and without a similar condition including this condition being imposed on the subsequent purchaser. Under no circumstances may any part of this book be photocopied for resale.

Although every precaution has been taken to verify the accuracy of the information contained herein, the author and publisher assume no responsibility for any errors or omissions. No liability is assumed for damages that may result from the use of information contained within.

The text of this book is composed in Roboto Slab and Bitter, with the headings set in Roboto and Roboto Condensed. Bitter was designed by Huerta Tipográfica and is used under the SIL Open Font License. All Roboto fonts were designed by Christian Robertson and are used under the Apache 2.0 License.

*For my wife, Sara,
and my children, Hanna and Leah*

Acknowledgements

Much like the process of successful test preparation, writing *Great Expectations* has been a thoroughly collaborative endeavor. For their wise suggestions and support, I am indebted to the entire CATES team: my staff, Adam, Daria, Howard, Iain, Jacci, Jason, Michele, Paige, and Ryan, as well as all the wonderful CATES tutors whose dedication to helping students succeed provides daily inspiration. I would also like to thank CATES's network partners, particularly Lisa Montgomery of Edvice, Michael Muska of Relativity College Consulting, and the staff of the Sutton Trust/Fulbright US Program, whose keen insights on all things admissions-related permeate the pages of this book. Most of all, I would like to thank each and every student I have worked with over the last 15 years. You have been my greatest teachers and, without you, this book would not have been possible.

Contents

Introduction 1

1. Realities of Testing 7
    Importance 7
    Sophistication 9
    Commitment 10
    The Truth About Scores 11
    The Wider Debate 15

2. Setting Goals 18
    The Vision 18
    Scores, Schools, and Fit 21
    Expected Results 23

3. Planning 26
    Start Early 26
    Plan for Multiple Tests 30
    Know "the Math" 31
    Scheduling Tips 35
    The Myth Behind Timelines 38

4. Essentials of Test Prep 42
    Three Skills of Successful Test-Takers 42
    Strategy Essentials 46
    Test-Taking Skill Essentials 53
    Mock Tests 55
    Test Day Essentials 57

5. Navigating the Process 61
Working With a Tutor 61
Barriers to Success 67
Parenting Cues 77

Conclusion 82
Your Roadmap 82
The Guarantee 83

Appendix 86
Overview of Tests 86
SAT vs. ACT Guide 88
SAT Subject Tests 92
Case Studies 99
Scoring FAQs 111
Myth & Reality for International Students 114
Best Practices for Institutions 118

About CATES 120
Who We Are 120
Methodology 120
Our Model 122
CATES Core 123
Institutional Programs 125
Team 127
Contact Information 128
Author: 129

Introduction

We live in a world of possibility. To be successful is to acknowledge this fact, one that applies as much to standardized tests like the SAT and ACT as it does to achieving in school, excelling at work, and leading a fulfilling home life. Success in standardized testing requires adopting a certain mindset: students, you must trust that you have the capability to succeed, and you must truly dedicate yourselves to the necessary preparation; parents, you must demonstrate no less of a commitment—to supporting and truly believing in your child, no matter the ups and downs that this process will inevitably bring. This commitment is what can make standardized testing so intense, but it's also what allows it to be empowering. At its best, the process creates a space for high schoolers to figure out how best to embody their ideal identities, providing for many students one of their first opportunities to cultivate the skills needed to creatively problem-solve and, most critically, to develop self-discipline.

I will return to the theme of self-discipline several times throughout this book. Why? Simply put, it's the key to success in virtually all arenas of life. By developing this skill now, students will set themselves up to succeed not only on test day, but well beyond. As any adult can attest, life presents a constant stream of crises and problems, like waves crashing on a beach. Whether you arrive home to realize you're locked out of the house, your professor announces a pop quiz that will make up 20% of your grade, or one of your top clients suddenly moves up the deadline for a branding campaign by two weeks, we are continually asked to deal with pressurized, high-stakes affairs in short time frames. To make the most of these situations, we must use our talents to navigate challenges in a fashion aligned with our larger goals. As well as describing life, this *is* standardized testing, whatever the test. (And there are many: head to the Appendix for a comprehensive overview of the testing landscape.) Taking any standardized test involves confronting problems that might seem intractable in the moment and that must be solved quickly and calmly. That's why, unlike any other academic assessments or exams, standardized tests require a unique type and degree of preparation and offer a uniquely transferable value proposition for students.

Students, over the coming chapters, I will share the secrets of how to guarantee you maximize your scores on test day. Doing so requires more than simply coming to grips with the academic concepts on the test; that's why this book will help you to build and improve all three components of successful test-taking: Content, Strategy, and Test-Taking Skill. Most students (as well as most tutors and prep providers) understand the need for content mastery, and even for appropriate testing strategies. But test-taking skill often remains overlooked or underdeveloped, a situation which time and again proves detrimental to students' scores.

Speaking from my own admissions experience, as an A-student in high school who went on to attend a top college, I initially found standardized tests to be quite challenging. On my first test, in fact, I went *down* by 20 from my PSAT scores. I faced real difficulties with timing and with maintaining the necessary focus over the course of the exam—and, frankly, during preparation, to which I gave barely a lick and a promise.

Growing up on Long Island, I'd taken a prep class at CW Post College on Sunday mornings. I sat in the back of the room and didn't pay much attention. My parents also hired a tutor, a family friend who was the Vice Principal at a local high school and a trained math teacher. He taught me the SAT Math, but in a way that didn't really suit my thinking, or even how it was tested on the exam. I remember sitting in my parents' car on the way to the test, trying to keep a calm exterior while I was freaking out inside. I felt physically sick. Indeed, it's an experience I recall to this day.

Yet even after the first test, I didn't do any real work (including with the tutor) to prepare myself for the next test as I truly needed to. In hindsight, I recognize that I suffered from what I now describe in my students as "smart kid arrogance." It's a dangerously easy problem to develop: after all, if your performance in school is excellent—perhaps even without much effort—why wouldn't you do just as well on the test? This way of thinking, however, simply does not honor the sophistication of the testing experience—and students who fall into this trap risk missing out on their full potential. This was the story of my own high school experience. I ended up with "good scores" and "good grades" and went to an excellent university, but I could have set myself up for greater success.

Ultimately, my scores improved, but not so much because of the test prep. It was only once I began to focus on the element of the testing experience that I now refer to as test-taking skill that I began to see substantial improvements. Years later, after I started working as a tutor (both independently and at a private firm in NYC), I saw many of my students encountering similar challenges to those I had once faced, yet the available solutions remained lacking. Only once I helped my students understand and accept the multifaceted nature of the testing experience did they reach their potential.

Indeed, the time in my life when I truly made up for my "deficiencies" in test-taking only came more recently, when I took the GRE. Given that I tutor students for grad school tests with a high degree of success, the content and strategy were not going to be a problem. Instead, it was going to be "test taking." The experience felt a little like being back in my parents' car 25 years earlier—but I was no longer "freaking out." I understood the context, the role of scores in the process, and the specific scores I needed to demonstrate ability within this context. And, of course, I was older. That said, despite my developed expertise, I still needed to work on timing, I still needed to do mock tests, and I still needed to manage myself during the unknown. I felt the pressure of the test itself, but also pressure of another kind: I *had* to do well because of my profession and my reputation within it. It goes to show that even when you're at an advanced level in any regard, you must still develop and maintain great technique and powers of self-regulation to successfully navigate the process.

INTRODUCTION

For students today, even before you master the three components of successful test-taking, there's an important—and often overlooked—first step. In my opinion, the best part of standardized testing (and, ultimately, the college admissions process) is that it requires students to ask themselves perhaps the most fundamental question a human being can ask:

Who do I want to be?

Sincerely considering this question, before you begin preparing for the test, sets the tone for everything that follows. Remember, high test scores are only a means to an end. Instead of trying to drive yourself with empty goals like "scoring well," or even "getting into XYZ school," invite yourself to envision who you want to be in the future, what impact you wish to have on your audience or community, how your future life will look, and what steps you must take now to attain it. This motivating vision provides the foundation for success with your academics, school choice, application strategy, college experience, career trajectory, and beyond. It also underlies successful test prep. Many students—including highly intelligent ones—don't do as well as they could on the SAT/ACT because they lack the drive that only this vision can truly provide. Conversely, many students who struggle in a traditional classroom context can do better than they expected on the test because they *do* possess this vision, and they allow it to inspire them towards success in preparation and on test day.

To be successful in testing, and elsewhere, you must have the self-awareness and determination required to take control of your own narrative. This is true for all students, but especially for those who are starting the process with a weaker academic profile. If you want to make the most of the advice in this book, you must willingly suspend all disbelief about your abilities. I don't care what you've been told before or what your personal history says about you—that's all in the past. I will assume capacity on your end, as we do with every student we encounter at CATES. As we progress, you must dig deep into a part of yourself that you may not have visited for a while: your personal genius. We meet this person through play, through games, and through all the exciting challenges in life that make our hearts flutter and our juices flow. Tap into the person you've imagined yourself to be in your dreams, the hero you've always wanted to be for yourself and for others. That's where we want to start. That's the energy that you need to channel. That's where this book begins: your ideal self.

Good luck,

Chris Ajemian

– 1 –
Realities of Testing

Before we embark on your journey to SAT/ACT success, you should understand the realities of the road ahead. Perhaps unsurprisingly, given the stakes of these tests, a number of myths and half-truths surround the standardized testing process. A quick search for "how to prepare for the SAT" will yield a web of contradictory advice on how schools view the tests, the best prep methods, how long preparation should take, what different scores mean, and so on. What's more, students today are confronted not only with questions on how best to prepare themselves for the testing experience, but also by larger debates surrounding the value and fairness of standardized testing itself. It's a lot to digest, and it can easily feel overwhelming to students who arrive at the process without clear guidance. My advice? Filter out the noise and focus in on the critical realities of testing outlined below.

Importance

Although most schools remain tight-lipped on precisely how scores factor into their admissions decisions, my professional experience tells me that standardized test scores are, without doubt, a significant determining factor in college admission. In fact, in 2016, over 80% of college counselors acknowledged the significant role test scores play in their admissions decisions, with almost 55% attributing "considerable importance" to scores.[1] What's more, these figures have barely changed in the last decade[2]—despite the increasing opprobrium directed toward standardized testing by skeptics and the rise of "test-optional" admissions. All in all, I've found that test scores are typically the second most important aspect of an application, after school grades. This is not *only* because schools are looking for bright students; colleges need to recruit students with good test scores, specifically, so that they can compete on the rankings tables and (further) enhance their prestige. Most colleges will say that they "look at the whole student," and, in my experience, they certainly do; but remember that a large part of that whole is the test score.

What does this mean for you? In short, take what admissions officers say about score ranges with a grain of salt. Having a high volume of applicants is great for schools, regardless of whether those applicants have a realistic chance of admission. For a start, more applications means more money collected in application fees; a 2017 study suggests that US colleges generate over $200 million from rejected applications each year.[3] Just as importantly, more applications usually means a lower overall admission rate, which in turn helps schools to increase their position on most major college rankings. And in our brand-driven attention economy, we can hardly blame the

---

1. Clinedinst, M., Koranteng, A. "2016 Admissions Trends Survey." *2017 State of College Admissions.* NACAC, 2017, p. 17.
2. 60% of counselors surveyed attributed "considerable importance" to test scores in 2006. Data from: *Report of the Commission on the Use of Standardized Tests in Undergraduate Admission.* NACAC, 2008, p. 22.
3. Gupta, V. "College Applications: A Huge Waste of Family Money." *UCEazy*, April 2017.

colleges for acting in this way. The truth is that all businesses and organizations—in order to survive and thrive—have to market and brand themselves in the best possible light. As smart consumers, whether of cars, iPhones, or college degrees, we have to understand and navigate this world in a manner that allows us to effectively further the goals of ourselves and our wider communities.

So next time you hear an admissions officer claim that test scores aren't the be-all and end-all of college admissions, acknowledge that this *is* true, to an extent. But know full well that the last time Duke accepted a student with SATs in the 500s was probably when they recruited that very nice young man who stood 7'1" and could dunk.

Sophistication

Hear, understand, and respect the reality: this is a sophisticated testing experience and it requires a sophisticated approach and strategy. These exams are challenging, and—straight-A students, take note—in ways far beyond simply grasping the material on the test. A weeklong course one week before the test simply does not cut it for new test-takers. Despite the ever-present critics of standardized testing in college admissions (a matter I discuss further in "The Wider Debate" below), the truth is that these exams do measure and require a specific type of intelligence. Beyond mastering the applicable academic content, they require great mental agility: the ability to think quickly and make fine distinctions, to recognize and apply the best strategies in a given situation, and to recognize and overcome the test-makers' attempts to confuse or misdirect students with tricky questions and subtly misleading answer choices. (And, before you wonder if I am unfairly disparaging the test-makers with this comment, know that they *readily admit* to doing this—it is, at the end of the day, a ruthlessly efficient method for separating competent students and thinkers from extraordinary ones.)[4]

Ultimately, successful test-takers understand that these exams require a certain attitude and approach to succeed. We'll get to the nuances of the tests and proper preparation later, but, for now, accept that the SAT and ACT are not simply another high school final, and that those who treat them as such will have difficulty finding the success they deserve.

Commitment

Many students don't improve as much as they could for a very simple reason: they aren't fully aware of what is necessary to succeed and how to improve. Many students think that they can do well on standardized tests because "they're a good student" or that they can "just do the course offered at school" and do well. Admittedly, this approach works for some—maybe .001%. The rest of us (me included) need to do it the proper way. And, by that, I mean we need to prepare, prepare, prepare. Would you walk into your biggest sales call or job interview without rehearsing your pitch? Would you prepare for the NYC marathon by taking a few laps around the track the

---

4. For instance, Anthony P. Carnevale, the former VP of Public Leadership at the Educational Testing Service (ETS)—that is, the makers of the SAT and GRE—noted in the 2018 documentary *The Test and The Art of Thinking* that, "In order to be efficient with the test, we essentially have to set out to trick people."

day before? *Hell no.* Standardized testing is no different. It's a learnable skill, but you must allow yourself the time to learn, unlearn, relearn, and learn again before you're actually able to absorb it and then (finally, on your second, third, or even fourth attempt) apply it fully on test day.

There is no magic pill for standardized test preparation, but there is a magic process, and you either commit to it or you do not. Successful test-takers treat the test as another advanced level class. It is still possible to succeed if you go about the process at less than 100%, but your chances diminish significantly—by more than half, in my opinion. Conversely, is it possible that you *won't* succeed if you *do* fully commit to the process? Highly unlikely. In my experience, no one works that hard for that long and fails to get their scores—provided that the work is of the highest quality (see "The Myth Behind Timelines" in Chapter 3). The only time it doesn't work out is when a student has truly out-sized goals that seem very unlikely based on the assessment and performance data.

The Truth About Scores

Before we start, let's define some important terms:

- **Diagnostic test:** The initial assessment to determine standing, strengths, needs, and test fit.
- **Practice test:** A test the student completes outside a "mock" testing center. Students typically complete practice tests in the comfort of their own home.
- **Mock test:** A test taken at a "mock" testing center—an office, classroom, conference room—alongside other

students and under the supervision of a proctor administering the experience under official test guidelines.

Test Scores Lie

Virtually all test prep journeys begin with a diagnostic test, which results in a diagnostic test score. All too often, we place too much emphasis on a diagnostic score (as well as later practice, mock, and real test scores). In truth, the score, diagnostic or otherwise, tells only part of the story. The most useful information lies not in the score itself but in the data and trends that led to that score. Making a judgement on how well a student has done or can do based solely on the numbers, particularly from a diagnostic or first test, does not respect the complete set of factors involved in the standardized testing experience.

Nowhere does this idea manifest more than in PSAT scores, an official examination within high schools that often acts as a student's "diagnostic." Every year, students and parents experience an emotion rather like sticker shock: "What?! My PSAT scores were what?" "You're an A student—your score should be higher!" When I encounter a family in this situation, I like to remind them that *test scores lie*. What do I mean by this? Simply that test scores, diagnostic and otherwise, often do not reflect the caliber of the student who attained them. While (in my opinion, at least) every student has "their" score, the journey to achieving that true score, for most students, is about erasing the difference between acting like an XX *student* and an XX *test-taker*—and there's a major difference.

What to Know About Lower Diagnostic Scores

For high schoolers, diagnostic scores stand as the most overblown component in the entire test preparation process. As noted above, diagnostic scores themselves are always less useful than the information that can be gleaned from mistakes made on the exam. In fact, I've found that lower diagnostic scores can be more helpful than higher scores (save for PSAT-takers aspiring towards a National Merit Scholarship).

What diagnostic scores (and, more so, the score reports) really provide is a peek into the student's mindset and level of mastery on the day of the test. That's all. PSAT scores, for instance, do not necessarily show a student's ability or a definitive prediction of the student's eventual SAT score. Rather, scores and score reports provide—after careful, insightful analysis—raw material that's invaluable in prioritizing how best to address the forces that influence students during the testing experience. Preparation can then focus on providing the student with whatever tools and resources are needed to ensure that these forces work in the student's favor on test day.

Moreover, lower-than-expected diagnostic scores provide an opportunity for students and families to learn how nuanced the standardized test preparation process can be. With lower-than-expected scores, students become more open to learning and understanding the realities of test preparation. And when parents discover the factors behind lower-than-expected scores, they may engage in the process in a healthier fashion, adopt smarter ways to support their child, and end up more likely to find success.

What to Know About High Diagnostic Scores

High diagnostic scores are great (of course), and high PSAT scores, specifically, can allow you to qualify for the National Merit Scholarship if you are a US citizen. This being said, many students who score highly on their diagnostic or PSAT can become over-confident. (This applies to the Aspire test, ACT's PSAT equivalent, too.) As a result, the openness we may see from a student with lower-than-expected diagnostic scores may not surface for a high-scoring test-taker. Students who do well on the diagnostic should take a moment to congratulate themselves for their early accomplishment, but they should remember, too, that there is still a long way to go. I urge you not to succumb to the same "smart kid arrogance" that, as I mentioned in the introduction, held back my own testing progress as a high schooler.

A practical advantage of high diagnostic scores relates to your high school college counselor. A counselor who sees high diagnostic scores from a student will naturally feel more comfortable recommending selective colleges. For a student with lower scores, the college counselor might not feel so confident encouraging the student to research selective institutions, regardless of how well the student performs in school. Of course, college counselors do understand that students seek support for test preparation and trust that the student will improve over time. You should be aware, however, that the first conversation or two with your counselor might not go as hoped. If you find yourself in this situation, be prepared to explain to your counselor why you feel that your diagnostic scores weren't where they could be, as well as what steps you are taking (such as taking a prep class or working with a tutor) to position yourself for better scores and thus more selective colleges.

The Wider Debate

Standardized testing in college admissions has a long and storied history in the United States, and the process has attracted its fair share of critics over the decades since the SAT first launched in 1926. Debates over their efficacy in measuring intelligence and college readiness are as old as the tests themselves. Today, these discussions have expanded to include questions about whether the tests produce equitable results for students from all backgrounds, among other issues.

In 2018, I was featured in *The Test and The Art of Thinking*, an SAT/ACT-focused documentary that explored some of these questions. Alongside me were several other tutors and education professionals, whose attitudes on the matter I found, for the most part, to be a touch pessimistic. To students reading this book, I urge you not to listen to such skeptical voices too closely. Of course, we must strive toward a system of educational assessment that gives each student a fair shot at success, and there are legitimate concerns that our current system does not achieve this. But for students going through the process *right now*, focusing too heavily on the problems with testing is counterproductive. With my students, I try to shift the conversation around testing away from "what's bad about it" and towards "the opportunity within it." Telling students that the test is bad, or worthless, or unfair simply does not help them to succeed. Rather, it preconditions students to have a bad experience with the testing process, creating anxieties and mental blocks that will hinder them on their road to success—and might cause them to miss out on the opportunities for growth that the current testing process *can* provide, if approached with the right mindset.

To reiterate, standardized testing is here and embedded in our educational culture. While I do not claim that the process is perfect, or even successful in producing its intended goals, it is here and likely to stick around for the foreseeable future. Thus, we simply have to face it. In this respect, I look at the SAT/ACT process like you might a Confirmation, Bat/Bar Mitzvah, or Quinceañera: as a rite of passage. Almost everyone will go through it, and if we approach the process with the right attitude and frame of mind, we can learn invaluable lessons about the way we think and manage challenges. Preparing for and taking the test demands our best: it teaches us how to set goals, strategize to achieve those goals, and manage obstacles along the way. We must learn new skills, break longstanding bad habits, and stop ourselves from falling back into these habits if thrown off our game. It's a matter of building an unshakable mindset and finding solutions when there seem to be no answers. That's very, very useful—for testing and for the myriad other challenges life throws our way.

All of this starts with one thing: believing it's possible. Too many people, in all aspects of life, carry a negative attitude into a challenge. It's simply impossible to succeed if you start off with anything less than a can-do attitude. When it comes to testing, improvement may not be easy, and it probably won't happen as quickly as you hope, but one of the reasons we've been able to help students achieve truly incredible score increases is because we have shown them, based on evidence, what is possible and we have reinforced that truth along the way. Whatever you believe to be true is your reality. You can make this process a dynamic, transformational experience—if you choose to.

– 2 –
Setting Goals

The Vision

Long-term, big-picture thinking makes a tremendous difference to your chances of finding success on the SAT and ACT. I cannot overstate the importance of setting smart, ambitious goals to motivate your testing experience. To do so, you must first ask yourself a question:

Who do you want to be?

It might seem simple, but in truth this question is as profound and complex as human existence itself. If you answer inauthentically—that is to say, if you allow external factors, whether parental expectations, school or peer pressures, or even "you from three years ago," to influence your decision—you're setting yourself up for disappointment and unfulfillment in the future. This is your life. Live it with agency.

So, truly, what is your vision of your ideal self? Where do you live? Who do you live with? How do you wish to spend your time (professionally and otherwise)? How much do you need to earn to live the lifestyle you desire? What impact do you wish to have on your community? Based on this vision of your ideal self, what schools or educational experiences would prepare you for that life?

If you're not sure, research people you admire in your possible fields of focus and learn about their paths. Remember, what is important might not be the specific schools they attended, but instead the particular experiences and opportunities they had through their schools. These opportunities may well be available elsewhere, and searching for them is a good way to find additional school choices. Which schools in the top 100 (on any rankings: US News, Forbes, etc.) provide opportunities for academic, extracurricular, and practical work experience to launch you into the career you desire?

Remember, too, that not everyone needs to go to college (right away, at least) to become who they want to be. Could an alternative educational experience better suit your needs? A good number of students don't head straight from high school to college. Some take informal gap years, others go through PG years or similar, and others still design custom experiences for personal development, perhaps to boost their skills or experience in a particular field. I've seen all of these options put into practice, and, provided that you have a clear plan for how this time will be used to further your future goals, they can represent a sensible and productive decision. Furthermore, depending on the future you envision, attending a four-year college might not be necessary at all. In recent years, several new options for high school graduates have arisen, such as MissionU, a career-oriented, one-year program designed to provide students with the skills and experience needed to launch directly into the job market. And, of course, more traditional alternatives, such as trade schools and apprenticeships, might remain the most viable path into the career you desire.

If this glut of options is starting to sound overwhelming, think of it like this: once you have a concrete idea of who you want to be, the path becomes clearer and simpler—all you need to do is what other "successful" people did (however you choose to define that term). Naturally, not every student will know who they want to be just yet; many will not even have been asked (or have asked themselves) the question. This is OK. Nobody expects 17-year olds to have everything figured out (and, in truth, those who do often change their minds later). But believe me when I tell you that *now* is the time to start thinking, if you haven't already.

If you are reading this book, I will assume that you do, in fact, wish to attend a selective college and plan to apply within the next year or so. If this sounds like you, once you have some schools in mind, you need to figure out their SAT and/or ACT score ranges. This data is available from a range of sources, including:

- Individual college websites
- BigFuture from The College Board
- US News College Compass (paid subscription)

Based on the school data, what kind of test-taker do you want to be on test-day? If you're taking the SAT, do you want to be a 1000+ test-taker? 1200+? 1400+? 1500+? And yes, I really do mean "want." Many factors work together to determine your scores, but *you are in control* of the vast majority of them. Whenever I ask students what score they think they can get, I always provide the same response: "You're right." My theory, based on over 15 years of professional experience, is that people get the score they *believe* they can get. And while we may not get there today, next week, or even next month, you need to remember that there is a way for you to get there.

Bear in mind, too, the difference between the scores students "want" to get and the ones they "need" to get in order to have a realistic shot at a particular school. You want to be at or above the 75th percentile for your school, but you *need* to be at or above the 25th percentile to be in range for the school. If you're not, your application efforts are probably best focused on a school with more achievable score ranges. By the way, "percentile" in this instance simply describes how your test scores compare to other students at a college—if your score stands at the 50th percentile at a school, for example, that means you scored higher than 50% of last year's freshman class.

Scores, Schools, and Fit

When thinking about which schools you wish to apply to—and thus what scores you need to earn—always place school fit above school prestige. That's right: Princeton (for instance) is not a great fit for every student. Many students fall into the name-brand trap and, in doing so, deny themselves the more valuable experience they might have found at a college more suited to them, whether in terms of location, size, academic support, extracurricular and professional opportunities, or so forth. Thus, students should be encouraged to seek a test score that is a true reflection of their innate ability, and let this guide them towards the schools that could best support their development. At CATES, we identify this "true" ability via carefully-constructed target scores, which we base on a holistic analysis of diagnostic test performance, a review of prior academic progress, and any number of qualitative factors that surface in our initial conversations with families. Ultimately, you should be looking for a school that best fits your needs as a student and as a person at this stage in your life. Wherever you end up, remember that you will be there for *four years*. The college you choose should be a place where you truly want to engage in the community, to challenge and be challenged by the environment and people around you. Thus, test scores that are a true reflection of your ability will help you determine in what range of schools (and communities) you might be happy.

Score Ranges

The following guidelines suggest which scores are likely to form part of a successful application to different categories of schools. Although, in my experience, these numbers generally hold true, keep in mind that there are exceptions to any rule: students with a 1590 SAT are frequently rejected by Harvard, even while some exceptional students with a "mere" 1420 sail through the ivy-clad gates.

- **1300/28+:** A student who aims for selective colleges (e.g. Indiana, American, Skidmore)
- **1400/30+:** A student who aims for more selective colleges (e.g. Michigan, NYU, Macalester)
- **1450/32+:** A student who aims for highly selective colleges (e.g. Boston College, UC Berkeley, Emory)
- **1550/34+:** A student who aims for the most selective colleges (e.g. Harvard, Stanford, Duke)

Score ranges from US News & World Report

Expected Results

Once students have some test scores in hand (whether from diagnostic or mock tests), they can begin to analyze their potential for improvement and use this information to make or refine school choices that are both ambitious and realistic.

How Much Can I Improve?

On average, students particating in a guided test prep program who start out with diagnostic scores of up to 20 on the ACT, or up to 1050 on the SAT, can expect an increase of up to 45% by the end of their program. Students with initial scores of up to 25 on the ACT, or up to 1230 on the SAT, may improve by closer to 30% from their diagnostic mock test. Students who begin with very strong diagnostic scores of up to 30 on the ACT or 1400 on the SAT are likely to see a more modest increase of around 15%.

The chart on the following page outlines these expected SAT/ACT score increases for the common categories of test-takers in CATES prep programs. Please do note that these ranges are anecdotal and cannot provide a guarantee for your individual score improvement. Although we've found these figures to hold true for a sizeable majority of our students, your eventual performance simply can't be boiled down to a set of data points—and if you encounter a prep program that tries to do so, I would urge you to treat it with caution. In my opinion, such promises simply don't respect the multifaceted nature of the testing process and, accordingly, the programs that make them usually aren't well positioned to help you earn the scores you could do, with the proper support.

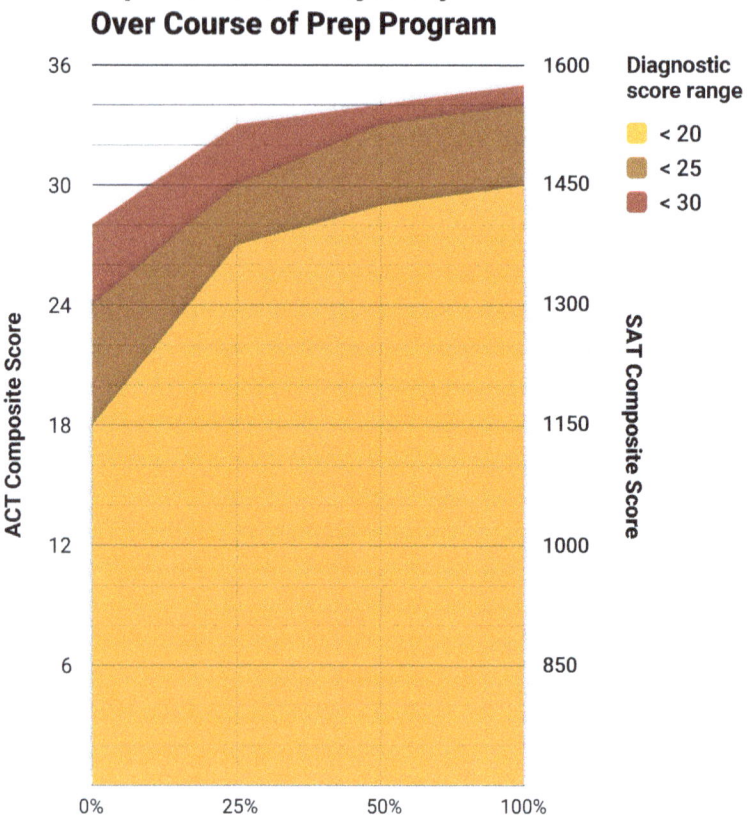

Students not participating in a guided test prep program usually see smaller score increases. The ACT estimates a 2-point score increase, for example, while the College Board estimates that students who complete their free SAT prep course will see an average 115-point improvement. Whatever preparation you plan on undertaking, your goal should be to finish the testing process with scores in (or exceeding) the middle 50th percentile for your top choice schools.

One Focus

As you finish setting goals for your standardized testing experience, do remember that this is only the first step. To maintain this momentum over the course of your preparation process will require genuine dedication (and, dare I say, passion) from you. It won't be easy. That's why the theme that ties all of this together, and the trait that should underpin all of your test preparation, is self-discipline. In fact, if I had to sum up the secret to standardized testing in a word, self-discipline would be it. No matter how smart you are, how many hours you put in, or how incredible your tutor is, self-discipline is what will ultimately determine your score.

Standardized tests do not always reward natural aptitude—at least, not to the extent that students might have experienced in other academic pursuits. The SAT, ACT, et al. demand careful, dedicated, and consistent practice and preparation, as well as spectacular endurance and focus during the test. You must decide upon a plan of study early, and you must stick to it all the way through to test day. In a sense, this entire exercise is more like athletic training than academics. When presenting in schools, I often point out that I am not a teacher, nor an academic coach—rather, I am a high-performance coach. Once you make the testing process about self-discipline, and allow this discipline to infuse all aspects of your preparation, it will allow you to apply laser focus to each section of the test, help you stick to a consistent preparation schedule, and give you the confidence needed to perform at the top of your game.

– 3 –
Planning

The high-stakes decisions involved in the test prep and college admissions process can challenge both students and parents. For perhaps the first time, students don't know what their next few years will look like, and their success is contingent upon several factors that might not play out as expected. But for those who plan ahead and fully commit to the preparation process, the risk of failing to secure a desired outcome is actually very low. Taking a leaf from the book of Brian Tracy, an acclaimed motivational speaker and author, I often tell my students that *success leaves tracks*. By this, I mean that high test scores cannot be produced out of thin air; rather, students who are successful have designed and *committed* to a complete, methodical plan of preparation.

Start Early

Most students learn that they cannot cram for standardized tests like they can for in-school tests. Many students learn this early in the process, but it takes them quite a bit longer to actually admit it—and ultimately accept it.

This is particularly true for strong students who are used to easily grasping challenging material in school. They come to the testing process with the attitude that they "already know this stuff" or that "I get everything else; I can get this easily, too." However, especially when the mock test process begins, students can find that their superpowers of academic performance aren't mature enough to stay fully focused over the course of a four-hour period. In other words, these students are succumbing to the same "smart kid arrogance" I described earlier.

This is an important moment in their preparation because, especially for these kids, they now see "what it's all really about." They are already great on the content and easily get the strategy, but are slow to come around to the fact that test-taking skill is the linchpin. Often, they are really held back by careless errors, born from a need for better focus within a section, general endurance issues, or a combination of both. Essentially, these students need to show the test more respect. It's a situation I encounter time and again (see Franco's case study in the Appendix, for example).

In a nutshell, once the student understands "the real challenge" on their own terms, generated from their own immediate experience with the obstacle (rather than a teacher or tutor telling them about it), they finally get it. But if students—and perhaps especially the best students—don't first leave themselves time to "fail," the chance that they will ultimately succeed is seriously diminished.

From a more logistical perspective, starting your standardized testing early goes a long way toward shortening the preparation timeline for future tests. This might mean a number of things—perhaps you take an SAT Subject Test in freshman or sophomore year, or perhaps you've prepared previously for the ISEE, SSAT, PSAT, or State Math/ELA exams.

One of my current students, Shari, credits her 1540 on the (Re-designed) SAT (Math: 800, Evidence-Based Reading + Writing: 740) to the foundational work we did in her sophomore year for the Chemistry Subject Test, on which she scored a 730. The same goes for her success on the Math Level 1 & 2 Subject Tests, on which she scored 780 and 760, respectively, with minimal additional support. The same logic held true for another student of mine, Katelyn. After spending much time together in 8th grade preparing for the ISEE, Katelyn returned for support with Subject Tests and AP exams in her sophomore year. With the foundation for success already laid by her previous preparation, Katelyn was able to score comfortably in the 700s on her Subject Tests with less than 15 hours of support, a feat which, particularly for a sophomore, represents a serious achievement. On top of this, she managed to score an *incredible* 34 on her ACT Diagnostic—with zero additional preparation—and closed out the process by scoring a 35 on her real ACT in September of her junior year with barely 10 hours of prep.

The moral of these stories is simple: by taking a test and getting good advice on how to approach test-taking early—while you probably have less going on in the way of school commitments, applications, and other tests—you give yourself the time and space to find prep methods that work for you, as well as to master key content knowledge and testing strategies that will, in many cases, continue to be applicable in the future. And, just like compound interest, this preparation goes on to produce higher scores down the road with vastly greater efficiency in terms of preparation time.

Start Early (Part Deux)

Even with the best-laid preparation plans, it can be easy to let the days (and weeks) slip by as you reassure yourself that you still have "plenty of time." Don't be this student. In case you needed any more persuasion, there are serious practical advantages to starting early:

1. Starting early diffuses the process. Preparation is more effective (and less likely to drive students and parents insane) when it happens in small, regular chunks.
2. It also allows the student to earn scores earlier in high school and thus provides space for more work on school assignments and college applications.
3. By starting testing early, you'll benefit from early score information, allowing for a more targeted school search process, which helps to organize college trips and manage travel budgets.
4. Starting early allows the student to adapt their preparation (e.g. different tutor, different approach, switch to a different test, extra attention on a specific content area) with enough time to do so while still feeling confident and in control of the process.
5. Most importantly, starting early helps the student feel ahead of the game and makes the entire process of college applications more manageable.

I tell students that it is never too early to start at least learning about how to navigate the process. While you may decide to learn about the testing process during your freshman year of high school but wait to start your formal preparation until the beginning of junior year, you can at least make that decision in an informed manner. You want to save yourself from the need to make decisions that you would not have made in hindsight "had I known then what I know now."

Plan for Multiple Tests

No matter who you are, you want to plan on taking the exam multiple times. In my experience, virtually all students, and particularly high-scoring students, take the test at least two times—and, in truth, probably three or more. As you can read in the student case studies, even high-scoring students who go to top universities give themselves a few shots at the tests.

Your first official test is likely to be the first stop on a larger journey of success. More often than not, success on SAT/ACT is not about how you start, but rather about how you finish. In fact, the first test is often simply about surviving—about knowing from first-hand experience that you can walk in (alive) at 8:30 AM and walk out (still alive!) at 1:30 PM. In doing so, you realize an important universal truth: the Boogeyman *does not exist.* This first exam provides great feedback, information, and context on how to help yourself succeed in the subsequent months. Thus, when you're planning your testing, plan conservatively (i.e. leave space for at least three tests) so that you have flexibility in your schedule. A lot can happen in a year, and you want to make sure that you have room to adjust along the way.

Know "the Math"

In reality, it takes most people about 100 hours of preparation (yes, really) to successfully achieve their scores on a standardized test, particularly one like the SAT or ACT. Here's why it takes such a long time:

1. Every program should start with a diagnostic test (four hours).
2. Students routinely put in 40–60 hours for the first official test, and then an additional 10–20 hours in preparation for each subsequent test. At CATES, we typically recommend that our students spend 30 minutes per day on test prep, six days a week, plus at least two hours with a tutor, bringing the total dedicated prep time to around five hours each week.
3. Most students take the test at least twice, if not three times. Many students take the test four or more times (including going into the test with the intention of cancelling the scores) as they feel that having as many reps as possible helps them master the testing experience. With our students, however, I've found that testing more than four times produces strongly diminished returns.
4. Students take anywhere from five to umpteen mock tests (including the diagnostic).
5. Extenuating circumstances, be it in school or at home, can delay or complicate timelines.

Of course, sometimes other commitments get in the way of students completing 100% of the work. This doesn't doom students to failure. But our metrics do show that the students who hit their target scores on their first test complete no less than 80% of the prescribed actions. Almost 95% of the students who complete 100% of the work hit their target scores on a first test.

Doing the Work: Question by Question

So what does "doing the work" mean in practice? We like to break this down for students into the number of questions they will need to complete with quality effort (be it in tutoring sessions, homework, practice tests, or mock tests) in order to achieve a particular goal. Doing so helps students see the scale of the work that lies in front of them (it's a lot!), but it also provides a quantifiable means to identify progress and a way to split that progress into achievable, bite-sized chunks. What exactly are those "chunks," and how many are there? It all depends on your goals:

IF YOU WANT TO:
Build Proficiency

You're probably starting the process fresh and looking to get comfortable with the tests in general, as well as the types of questions being asked and the ways you must apply the knowledge learned in school to the problems presented in the exam.

→ In **areas of strength** (usually non-Math), you should complete:
  - ✓ **120+ questions**, or
  - ✓ **480+ questions** (if you also need to get comfortable with the timing)

- In **areas of weakness** (usually Math), you should complete:
  - ✓ **600+ questions**, or
  - ✓ **1800+ questions** (if you also need to get comfortable with the timing)

IF YOU WANT TO:
Master Unfamiliar Content

You're likely already familiar with the format of the test and the categories of questions you'll be asked, and you've already started building your confidence in applying the appropriate strategies to different question types. Now, your goal is to plug any holes in your content knowledge that are holding back score improvement.

- How much work is required in this situation truly must be determined on a case-by-case basis, depending on any number of factors, including learning style, educational background, possible learning differences, executive functioning skills, and, most of all, commitment.

IF YOU WANT TO:
Develop Question-Specific Strategy

Your content knowledge is up to scratch but you can't seem to translate this expertise into sustained score increases. For you, it's time to learn how to think like the test-makers; or, put differently, you need to learn and practice question-specific strategies.

- In **areas of strength**, you should complete:
    - ✓ **120+ questions**
- In **areas of weakness**, you should complete:
    - ✓ **600+ questions**

IF YOU WANT TO:
Develop Question-Specific Strategy & Resolve Timing Issues

Does time frequently run out before you've completed the test? Can't figure out how other students put their pencils down five minutes before the end of a section while you're still scrambling to find the answer to Question 6? In this case, you probably want to focus on both question-specific strategy and timing. Timing on standardized tests is a tough nut to crack, but it is possible, for *every* student, with the right practice.

- In **areas of strength**, you should complete:
    - ✓ **480+ questions**
- In areas of weakness, you should complete:
    - ✓ **1800+ questions**
- For students who face timing challenges, it is crucial to work with a timing device, even during practice.

IF YOU WANT TO:
Develop Complete Mastery

You're looking to enter the big leagues—and take home the trophy. To do so, you must develop the absolute mastery over each element of test-taking (content, strategy, and test-taking skill) needed to hit your target score *consistently*, even during the high stakes of an official exam experience. Attaining this level of mastery is difficult and time-consuming, but it is what truly separates the amateurs from the pro test-takers—and, just maybe, what stands between you and the next stage of your educational career.

- → You should complete:
  - ✓ **1500+ questions**
- → In total, you should take no less than:
  - ✓ **10 full practice tests**
  - ✓ **10 full mock tests** (which should all be previously administered or "official" tests published by the test provider)

Scheduling Tips

As previously stated, long-term thinking about the preparation process proves to be critical. Students who begin their preparation by the end of sophomore year hit their target scores more frequently and earlier than those who do not. To see these principles in practice, take a look at the case studies in the Appendix.

The value of earning strong scores by spring of junior year cannot be overstated. Here are just a few reasons why:

Spring School Exams

Many schools, regardless of geography and education model, run fairly important exams in the spring. For example, some New York City private schools schedule their finals for March, while the College Board administers Advanced Placement (AP) exams globally in the first two weeks of May. Similarly, students taking IB or A Levels generally sit high-stakes mock exams in the spring that are used to generate grade predictions for colleges. In China and India, the Gao Kao and AISSE exams, respectively, are also administered in the spring months.

Thus, preparing for the ACT or SAT simultaneously only adds to the challenge. These factors explain why many students, despite their best efforts, do not score as highly on June SAT/ACT exams as they hoped. Because of this, it is strongly advisable to take the ACT or SAT before this period (or after—but heed the warnings below about overbooking your senior fall).

Senior Fall

Senior fall epitomizes the need for smart planning. Seniors must manage the start of school (unto itself "a thing"); fall sports commitments (especially pre-season matches, which tend to fall just when you thought you'd have spare time to finish your Common App essays); the completion of college applications, which includes finalizing essays and nailing down teachers for recommendations; any last school visits (particularly if you're still deciding to which school to apply early); a potential need to show strong senior fall grades to strengthen college applications; and everything else going on with your life, including holidays, weekend parties, and perhaps your birthday. In other words, seniors have *a lot* going on.

Thus, any fall testing can become challenging to schedule (whether last-chance SAT/ACT tests or SAT Subject Tests before the Early Action/Early Decision deadline, normally November 1). This being said, it's certainly possible to succeed on fall tests, and taking exams during the fall can become smart and necessary to position yourself for admission to your top choice school.

Generally speaking, I have found that students who take the exams in senior fall, particularly those who started in junior fall or spring, tend to do extremely well because their skills and psyche have had additional time to mature over the summer between junior and senior years. Indeed, some college admissions directors have said that they like senior year test scores because the student is likely "at the height of their educational development"—which I think is a great, true and valuable observation, as well as proof that admissions directors really do want to evaluate you on your strengths.

School Choice

Another reason you should aim to finish your testing before senior year is a more practical one: where are you applying? As previously stated, while test scores may not be able to get you into a school, they absolutely can keep you out. Thus, if you're not at least in range for your top choices (and by "in range" I mean with scores between the 25th and 75th percentiles of a school's published SAT/ACT score range), it can complicate matters of school choice and limit your options. This influences the viability of school visits and makes things harder on your college counselor (who really does want to help you get into the best fit school for you). It also creates a lack of clarity and direction at a time when you probably want to have a strategy in place for which schools you want to pour your heart, time, and energy into.

Thankfully, the ACT and the College Board now provide summer testing in July and August, respectively, to help ease the challenges of senior fall. Worth noting, however, is that this generosity currently only extends to students in the US. Those applying from abroad still must manage their timelines as if the July ACT and August SAT are not options—because they aren't. The September ACT and October SAT remain as the best options for "last chance" international seniors.

The Myth Behind Timelines

Although the guidelines above provide a good starting point, in truth, there is no perfect timeline for test preparation. In other words, there are as many timelines as there are students. In this process, the quality and consistency of the time you put in often bears greater potential for improvement than the raw quantity. And although it's important that students receive some input on how best to manage timelines, given their often CEO-esque schedules, how long a student ultimately takes to succeed on the test usually comes down to their own decision-making, their knowledge of the process, and their trust in their ability.

Alexandra: New York, 2007

I once helped a wonderful student in New York, Alexandra, who wanted to apply Early Decision to NYU. Alexandra was extremely bright and relentlessly driven, and she possessed all the capability necessary to succeed on the test. She was preparing for the (Old) SAT and needed to focus most on the Math. Her diagnostic score came in around 540, and we set her target score at 700 with complete confidence that she could nail it. Throughout the program, Alexandra did an excellent job of staying consistent and completing her homework. She became a model student and was on track to be a "One and Done" on the May SAT.

Alexandra's biggest needs came through on the mock tests. Like many students, she came face-to-face with the affective factors that can impede progress, which, in her case, meant careless errors created by rushing. The time spent during our sessions between March and late April centered continuously on one theme: "Each question counts the same. Every question matters." Alexandra tended to rush through to "get to the end of the section" so that she could score "more points." But in practice, the opposite was happening: she was missing early (easier) questions and those questions dramatically affected her score. Alexandra took so many mock tests that she maxed out our entire catalogue of exams at the time (more than 20), and she was either at 650 or 710. She was even higher on some tests.

We had the heart-to-heart; we had the coaching conversation; we discussed it all. When the May test came around, I told her that her mock testing had given us a history of proof. When Alexandra embraced—and trusted—the fact that she could do every question on the test, and gave every question her complete attention, she performed faster because she was testing with clarity. In doing so, she broke 700 each and every time.

Alexandra took the May test, earning a 670. "Terrific start," I told her. On the SAT, it's not uncommon for first-time testers to drop 30 points or so from their mock test medians due to environmental or affective factors on the day. Alexandra's numbers landed in that range, and, especially knowing how she at times struggled to handle her thoughts and emotions, I was proud of her. This was a great start and a real building-block for future testing.

When her May Question-and-Answer Service arrived in mid-June, we sat down together to review her question-by-question results, identify where we needed to further focus, and help her "complete the picture" of her scores in October.[1]

So, what happened? Alexandra missed the very first question in each of the four subsections on the Math portion of the Old SAT. Every first question: in the 20-question section, the 1–8 subsection of the 18 question section, the first Grid-In in the 18-question section, and the final, 16-question section. That's four raw score points, which amounted to 50 scale points. In other words, she could have scored a 720. Had Alexandra tested with better care and clarity, she would have not only met but exceeded her target score of 700 on her first test.

After reviewing the exam, Alexandra admitted that the stakes of the experience got to her and that she had fallen into her

---

[1]. The Question-and-Answer Service is offered by the College Board and provides students with a copy of the SAT questions and a report showing their answers from a specific test, along with the correct answers, additional scoring instructions, and information about the type and difficulty of test questions. The service is available for Saturday tests in October, March, and May for US and Canadian testers, but only in May for international testers. The Student Answer Service is similar, and available for all tests regardless of date or location, but it details only how you answered questions and the level of question difficulty—not the questions themselves, nor the correct answers.

pattern of "rushing to get to the end." In truth, this experience was a blessing in disguise for Alexandra, as she now fully accepted that the decision for how long she would need to prep for the SAT was in many ways up to her. She made the decision to close it out in October, and she did with a 740. The moral of Alexandra's story? Test prep doesn't always take a "fixed" amount of time, and only the student truly possesses the power to determine when they will allow themselves to perform at their best.

– 4 –
Essentials of Test Prep

Three Skills of Successful Test-Takers

Standardized tests, particularly due to their length, incorporate three elements: content, strategy, and test-taking skill. Successful test-takers have built confidence in each of these three domains, comprised of twelve sub-domains:

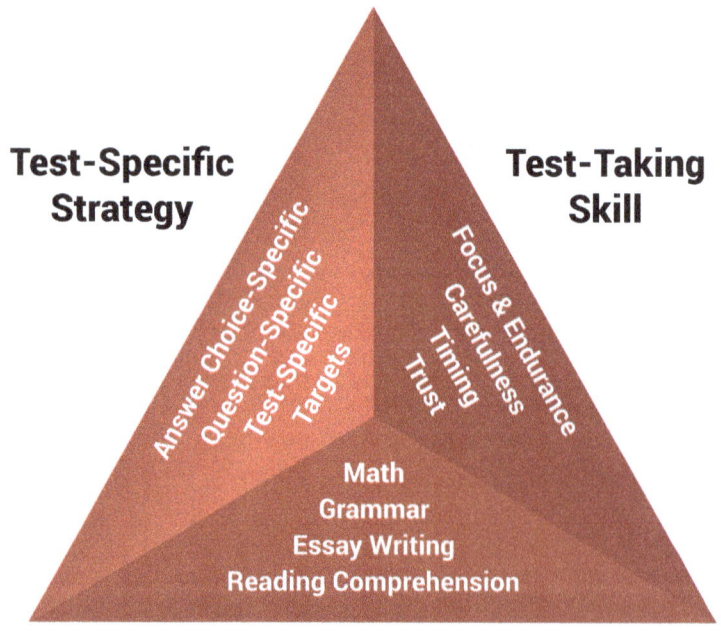

ESSENTIALS OF TEST PREP   43

Here's how achieving mastery over each domain typically affects students' scores over the course of a prep program:

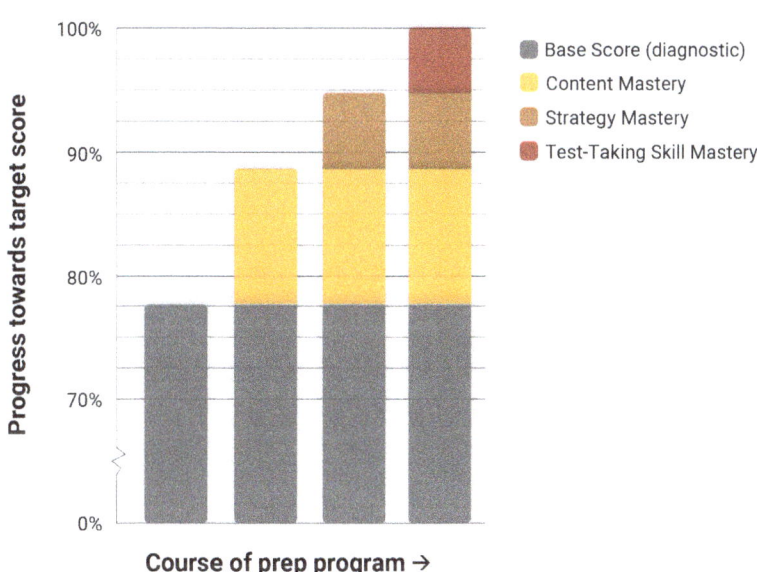

Domains of successful test-taking & progress toward target scores

- Base Score (diagnostic)
- Content Mastery
- Strategy Mastery
- Test-Taking Skill Mastery

Course of prep program →

Content

While plenty of students can boost their scores with smart tactics (and a little luck), everyone must know the content covered on the exam, inside and out, in order to maximize their performance. By "content," I mean the relevant academic knowledge, concepts, and skills in English, Math, Reading, Science, and Writing that are tested by the SAT and ACT. Both the College Board and ACT loosely align their test content with the Common Core standards, so, depending on your school's curriculum, most topics should feel at least somewhat familiar to you. Check for yourself in the table below, which outlines the primary tested subject matter within each academic domain for both the SAT and ACT.

SECTION	SAT	ACT
Critical Reading	Command of Evidence Words in Context Analysis in History/Social Studies	Key Ideas & Details Craft & Structure Integration of Knowledge & Ideas Understanding Complex Texts
Math	Heart of Algebra Problem Solving & Data Analysis Passport to Advanced Math	Number & Quantity Algebra Functions Geometry Statistics & Probability Integrating Essential Skills Modeling
English/Grammar	Command of Evidence Words in Context Expression of Ideas Standard English Conventions Analysis in History/Social Studies	Production of Writing Knowledge of Language Conventions of Standard English
Science*	Analysis in Science	Interpretation of Data Scientific Investigation Evaluation of Models Inferences & Experimental Results
Essay**	Reading, Analysis, & Writing	Ideas & Analysis Development & Support Organization Language & Conventions

* The SAT does not give a separate measure of Science ability as part of its composite. Rather, it gives a cross-test score which is reported as a separate marker on the score report.
** Both the SAT and ACT offer their tests with and without the essay. Often the writing is not required, but it is wise to confirm with your school(s) of choice.

Strategy

While knowing the content is an absolute must, in truth, content represents only a third of the task (albeit a "big third"). Students must also properly employ test-specific strategy. The approach to SAT Math, for example, differs from the approach to ACT Math, and both differ from the approaches to the SAT Subject Tests in Math Level I and Math Level II. Each of these exams is an entity unto itself, testing similar material in ways different enough to influence a student's strategy. "Strategy" means not only the tactics used to answer specific questions but also the student's personalized approach to the test as a whole: scoring, timing, and methods for choosing between two answer choices based on the conditions at play in the moment. Students who understand how to read and respond to the various test components stand poised to maximize their scores.

Test-Taking Skill

Even if a student has mastered the content and test-specific strategy, if they cannot stay focused consistently—over the course of four hours on the SAT or ACT, for example—the student will not maximize their score. Thus, "test-taking skill" refers to the set of skills related to timing and time management, focus (complete engagement with materials), endurance (maintaining focus over the course of four hours, if not more), carefulness (catching and correcting potential careless errors), and trust (faith your instincts are correct when handling the unknown). These soft skills are just as critical to success as the more quantifiable, cognitive skills related to content and strategy. Most often, the student's ability to develop strong test-taking skill is often the deciding factor in whether a target score is achieved.

Strategy Essentials

While this book focuses mainly on how to structure your journey to a guaranteed score, rather than acting as a more conventional "prep book," I would like to pass along what I refer to as "Your Three Best Friends" for the two more overlooked domains of standardized testing: Strategy and Test-Taking Skill.

The best friends all support you in your one and only task on the test: to eliminate what you know is wrong for a fact first, and then to choose the best of what's left. That's it. We're not looking for "the right answer"—indeed, we may never find one, at least to our personal satisfaction. We're simply looking to fill in the correct bubbles before the time elapses. To do so in the most efficient manner, we want to, again, *eliminate what we know is wrong*, for a fact, and then *choose the best of what's left*.

The following information will be of particular use to students who do not have access to additional resources or input on how to frame their approach to their test. Furthermore, while I will contextualize your "Three Best Friends" with respect to the ACT and SAT, I have found the same "friends" to prove trusty on virtually all standardized tests, from the ISEE/SSAT all the way through to the GRE, GMAT, LSAT, and MCAT. You might be on the verge of creating a friendship that lasts your testing lifetime.

English: Three Best Friends

Context, Context, Context

Context is king on this test. When I refer to "context", I mean the context of the words directly before and after the selection, the context of the sentences before and after the sentence within the selection, the context of the paragraph, and even the context of the passage as a whole, particularly for big picture questions. The correct answer will be the one that works with the ideas and concepts around it, i.e. the "context."

Independent vs. Dependent Clauses

If you can master the differentiation between independent and dependent clauses, and understand how changes to grammar and punctuation affect the independent and dependent nature of a clause, you can answer at least 60% of the questions tested and are 90% of the way toward an elite score. Understanding the difference between independent and dependent clauses, and the related punctuation rules, may be the single most effective skill to learn for the Critical Reading and English sections on the SAT and ACT.

"Ye Olde British Dude"

The Old British Dude, aka "The OBD," is the stereotypical old English professor who's pretty cranky about grammar. She or he is not someone that we're hanging out with on Saturday night, but we do need to know how they like and write their English. The OBD is your best friend when checking your answer choices against the context of the sentence, especially when you mutter those often fateful words, "That sounds like how I'd say it." In these times of possible misstep, the OBD will straighten you out. The OBD's eye for grammar, and not your (teenage) ear for "what sounds right to me," is the standard for the test. Remember the OBD.

Reading: Three Best Friends

The Questions

The reading test has three primary components: the text, the questions, and the answer choices. Of these, the questions are the most important element. Regardless of whether or not you read the text before answering the questions, let the questions lead your thinking and direct your approach regarding how to treat and break down text, which solution strategy to employ for the specific question, and how to eliminate answer choices for the question type. The questions also provide guidance for how to choose the correct answer when down to two.

The Theme

It's critical to understand the theme of the passage. Theme (or, more specifically, "What the author wants you to know about the topic") sets the frame of context for eliminating answer choices. For many questions, particularly "Big Picture" questions, if the answer choice does not support or align with the theme, it's incorrect. How do you identify the theme? Easy: simply reread the first two sentences of each paragraph, as well as the final sentence of the entire passage.

The Tone

Although tone plays a smaller role in certain kinds of passages (e.g. science-oriented passages, which remain somewhat objective), it's certainly one of your best friends. As with theme, if an answer choice does not support or align with the the author's tone (or, more specifically, "How the author feels about his or her attitude toward the topic"), the answer choice is likely incorrect.

If you struggle to identify the author's tone—and most students do—you want to focus on the individual words the author uses to build her argument or describe her thoughts. This normally comes down to identifying the adjectives and verbs the author chooses to use. For example, "The boisterous home crowd cheered after Jones scored the winning goal" and "The nervous home crowd deflated after Jones scored the winning goal" are tonally quite distinct and thus paint two very different pictures regarding Jones's goal. The adjectives and verbs indicate the tone and, in this case, communicate different ideas about the meaning and implications of the sentence. In the first sentence, for example, we could reasonably infer from the tone that Jones is a player on the home team, whereas the opposite would be true for the second sentence.

Math: Three Best Friends

Strategy vs. Content

While you absolutely must learn the relevant Math concepts, strategy is just as important as the content itself in maximizing your Math score. This remains the case even as test-makers such as the Educational Testing Service (which makes the SAT, on behalf of College Board, as well as the GRE) attempt to make the questions more content-based. When test day arrives, the real question to answer remains "What's the best way to approach this?"

As such, you want to make sure that you memorize and master the common general solution strategies so as to answer each question as efficiently as possible. If you came to a square-shaped park with a nicely cultivated path along its perimeter, but needed to cross to the opposite corner as quickly as possible, would you take the path? No way. You'd cross the green on a diagonal to get directly to your destination. The same holds true for testing. For SAT and ACT Math, your strategic arsenal should include the following:

Just do the math:

Often, simply performing the calculations normally involved with the concept does prove to be the simplest and most efficient strategy.

Plug in:

Also referred to as "Use Numbers" or "Make it Real," this strategy applies to questions that feature variables and involves simply replacing the variables with actual numbers and solving from there.

Backsolve:

Some people call this "Backtracking." Here, use the values given in the answer choices and work backwards to see which one solves the problem.

Draw it out:

Simply drawing your own figure, chart, or graph can be vital for geometry questions, particularly ones that do not provide a figure to begin with.

Use the calculator:

For many tests, you have powerful device at your side (or, in the case of the GRE, embedded into the toolbar). Don't forget to make use of it. The calculator is particularly helpful for graphing questions.

Use a chart:

Although I'm not personally a fan, many students find that using a chart is helpful for solving percentage and rate questions.

Use the given formulas:

In some cases, the question provides a formula related to the problem. Use it. The formula would not be there if it weren't needed to solve the problem.

Use your pencil as a ruler:

Unless otherwise indicated, all figures on the exam should be drawn to scale. Thus, if you're in a bind or the question doesn't seem to give you enough information to find a length or the distance between two points, use your pencil to answer the question. To do so, use the confirmed lengths or distances in the given shape or figure, mark that measure on your pencil with your fingernail (or perhaps relate it to letters within the brand name impressed in the pencil), and then match that measure, as if your pencil were a ruler, against the unknown to estimate the unknown value. While inexact, this tactic will likely help you eliminate incorrect answer choices and get them down to at most two choices, if not the correct choice.

Guess:

Especially for tests where you do not lose points for incorrect answers (which now means both the SAT and ACT), simply guess—never leave a question blank.

Thinking on Paper

On to your second best friend in Math: thinking on paper. Whether you're taking a computer- or paper-based test, you need to "think on paper." The test-makers are extremely smart and they understand deeply how test-takers think during the exam experience. Questions, particularly the more challenging ones, are phrased in a specific manner to challenge your ability to understand them with only a cursory read. Break questions down into smaller pieces, write out implied information, and perform calculations on paper (even the smallest ones) to ensure you work with clarity. Doing so increases your chances for catching and correcting careless errors. I also tell students that, be it in the Math or otherwise, the more you write down on the paper, the higher your score—and the more math you do in your head, the lower your score.

The Calculator

Again: you likely have use of a powerful device during the exam. Use it. Check simple calculations; perform complicated calculations; graph functions. Of course, you want to do these things efficiently so the calculator does not have the reverse of the intended effect and slow you down. That takes practice. Finally, for some students, particularly those who are still in the process of building confidence with the math, here's some advice: do what you can to use the calculator as much as possible. Ask of each question: "What must I do in order to use the calculator to answer this question?" This thinking normally leads you to approach the question from a more strategic standpoint (i.e. Plug in, Backsolve, Use a formula) and thus simplifies how to answer. And this approach works. In fact, a student of mine who *really* struggled with Math improved her ACT Math score from 18 to 29 after committing to this approach—which, in turn, helped her earn early admission to UPenn.

Test-Taking Skill Essentials

In addition to those I introduced in the "Strategy" section above, please allow me to introduce your "Three Best Friends" within the domain of test-taking:

Your Pencil

We have already discussed how your pencil can be used as a ruler, as well as the importance of "thinking on paper," which applies to every section on the exam. Additionally, the pencil provides an easy way to boost your score immediately by helping you to eliminate a primary cause of students not reaching their target scores: careless errors.

The pencil acts as antidote to these errors because you can use it to "circle the details." (Note that I say "circle" and not "underline"—although the techniques seem similar, I've found circling to be far more effective with my students). Circling important details (such as facts, figures, and key terms) helps to reduce careless mistakes because doing so ensures that your focus is "locked in" and that you are working with care and clarity over the course of the whole test. We've seen this technique take students from 30 to 34 on the ACT and from 1300 to 1500 on the SAT literally overnight.

Your Watch

Work with a timing device. Make sure you set clear intervals within which to work and that you practice hitting your target scores consistently within those time intervals. Break the test down one section at a time and drill timing on the individual sub-sections, passages, or units. As you use the watch more and more, you'll become naturally conditioned to perform at your desired pace. Also, choose no more than two or three times to look at your watch (or the clock on the wall). I normally recommend that students check their watch half-way through the section and then again three-quarters of the way.

Your Snack

Eating properly is also vital—nutrition plays a huge part in test-taking. Make sure that you have a full breakfast before the test, and, just as importantly (and all too often overlooked), be sure that you have a snack during the first break of the test. This infusion of energy will kick just as your breakfast wears off and will help you push through the last few hours of the exam. On test day, choose foods with a low glycemic index (i.e. slow-release sugar) which will help to keep you energized and focused over the full four-hour experience. A wide array of foods will serve you well here. For breakfast, consider foods like oatmeal (non-instant), bran, or unsweetened yoghurt. For your snack, various fruits, like apples, grapes, oranges, and cherries have a low GI, as do other trusty snacks such as peanuts and seed mixes.

Mock Tests

Live, in-person mock tests are crucial to developing the "soft" test-taking skills described above, as well as to identifying any problems in content or strategy. Overall, they prove time and again to be the most critical factor in standardized test preparation. Many students see a drop of around two points on the ACT, or 30–50 points on the SAT, in their first official test. The reason for this fluctuation is nearly always the same: the student lacked practice in applying their technique during the high-pressure exam experience. The students who ultimately score closest to their medians are the ones who take the most mock tests, and the more the better. The data is unequivocal on this point. The chart on the following page shows an example from one of my students, Edward, who ended up going to Penn after being admitted in the Early Decision round.

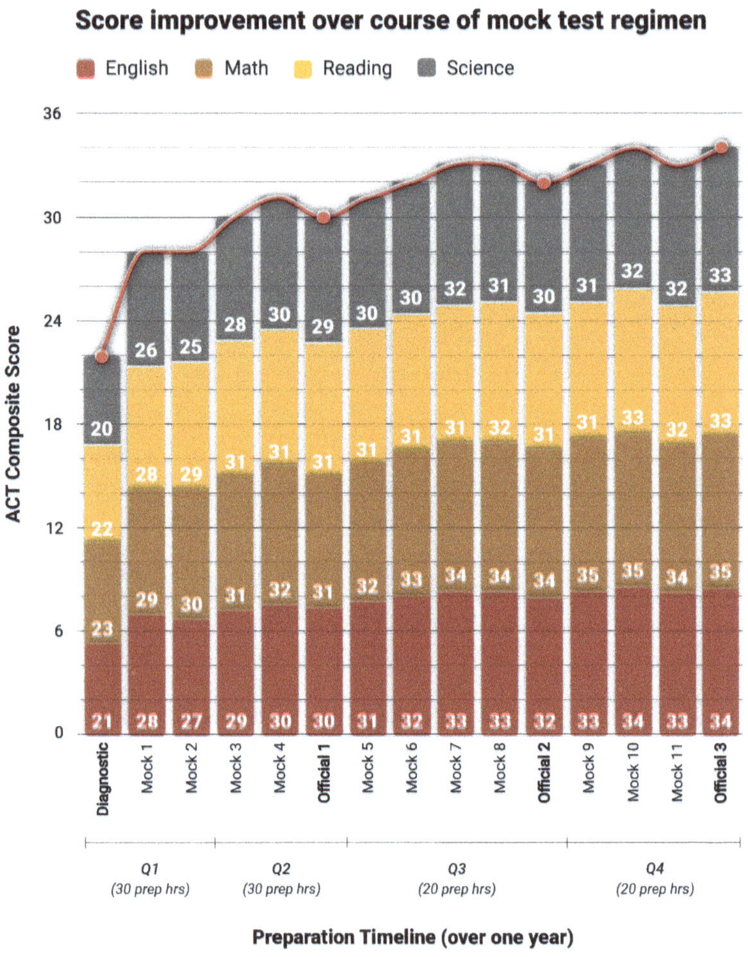

As you can see, Edward saw significant score jumps as his mock testing continued and, in the end, he scored slightly above the average of his last three mock tests. Generally, we find that these later mock tests are crucial in insulating students from significant score drops on test day. The data also reveal another common trend: students tend to experience quick starts and plateaus, and the final 20% of their preparation can take nearly as long as the first 80%. Ultimately, mock tests prove to be the best way of getting over the hump and achieving target scores.

Real Tests

CATES only evaluates progress based on students' performance on real, released or retired tests (i.e. genuine SAT/ACT exams, written by the test-maker) for mock tests and benchmark exams. Why? It's only truly possible to gauge students' progress on real tests, taken under real testing conditions.

Material made by a test prep provider, such as McGraw Hill or Princeton Review, doesn't provide students with an accurate measure of their progress due to variations in difficulty and question style. Students who rely on these practice tests risk becoming over- or under-confident, either of which can prove fatal on test day. Material from test prep providers should be used for practice and to work out issues related to content, strategy, and test taking, while real tests should be reserved for measuring progress. Consider this factor as you plan your preparation and mock test schedule, because these real tests can be hard to come by—the only legitimate sources are the test-makers' official prep books.

Test Day Essentials

Breathe & Reboot

If you can control your breath, you can control yourself. Many students forget to breathe during the exam and, as a result, do not think as clearly as they could.

Why is this so important? Controlling your breathing is a proven strategy for reducing tension, and it can help you to focus your mind on the task at hand. Refresh your mind during the exam by taking three deep breaths at the beginning of each section to focus and center yourself. Take another breath at the middle of the section to refocus. Practice this at home, at school—or anywhere. Additionally, don't be afraid to do some yoga, jumping jacks or any other activity during the exam (probably on the breaks, and not during the sections!) to reboot and refresh your mind.

Keep to Yourself

Don't talk to anyone once the exam has started. Although it might be hard to ignore any friends outside the exam center, in the hallways beforehand, or when you're getting settled into your seat, keep to yourself as soon as official procedures begin and all the way through to the end of the last section.

This is especially true for the bathroom breaks. Don't engage with other students who ask what you got for a certain question or how you think the test is going. Students' experiences and results vary greatly on test day and students often aren't accurate predictors of their performance. Don't get caught up in what others report —good or bad—as it has nothing to do with you and your own performance.

This advice may seem a little draconian, but, in the pressurized testing atmosphere, even a small knock to your confidence can harm your performance. If a conversation with other test-takers leads you to negatively appraise your chances of success on the test, you may face increased test anxiety and other emotional roadblocks that will distract you from achieving your potential score.

So keep cool, keep composed, and keep to yourself. If you do choose to talk to someone, talk about something other than the test.

Play to Win

As we have discussed, you want to embody the identity of your "ideal self" on test day. But simply existing within that mindset is not enough: you need to activate it. We remind our students that there's only one way to play the game—play to win.

Too many students play "not to lose," and, in doing so, they are playing in fear: fear of making a mistake, not doing the right thing, or messing up. Consequently, these students become preoccupied with regulating their emotional state rather than devoting full focus to the task.[1]

When we "play to win," however, we play with love, passion, and complete confidence. Yes, we will fall. But we will stand back up. Yes, we will be imperfect. But nobody is perfect. And while we might play imperfectly, we can still play spectacularly. You've put in too much work and come too far to allow fear or resistance to overcome you. Play to win and you'll slay

---

1. For a more academic take on this process, see the research article below, which explores the links between 'Task Focusing Processes,' 'Emotion Focusing Processes,' and 'Cognitive Appraisal Processes' in a testing context and how these factors combine to influence students' performance:

    - Schutz, P. "The Emotional Regulation During Test-Taking Scale." *Anxiety, Stress & Coping: An International Journal*, vol. 17, no. 3, 2004.

any inner dragons to not only embody your desired identity on test day but also to act within it—and succeed.

– 5 –
Navigating the Process

Working With a Tutor

Many, many students work with tutors on their test preparation—from the SHSAT/ISEE, through the SAT, ACT, Subject Tests, and AP exams, all the way to graduate tests like the GRE, LSAT, and GMAT. In our hypercompetitive education market, where most families are keen to secure a leg up in the admissions process, the reality is that students who *don't* work with a tutor of some sort are increasingly in the minority. Being a tutor myself, I am (naturally) inclined to believe that tutors can offer real benefits to students going through the testing process: besides the obvious advantages afforded by having an expert in the test content and strategy on hand, test prep tutors (or, at least, those who are true professionals) have real-world experience of what makes students tick and of what factors can impede score improvements—some of which might not be immediately obvious to students who are self-preparing, or even to other teachers or tutors who are not so well-versed in the intricacies of the test prep process.

This being said, hiring a tutor—as with hiring any other professional—is not a process to take too lightly. There *are* common pitfalls, and getting the best results will require research on the parents' part, as well as careful consideration of the student's needs. You want a tutor with experience and expertise, of course, but also one whose personality will mesh well with the student's, and one who is able to adapt and customize their teaching style, as well as the strategies and study methods they suggest, in line with the student's individual learning style and personal qualities—both of which, of course, might well evolve over the course of a tutoring program. You want the person who is going is going to be right for you at the beginning, middle, and end of the process. This reality is why we often see "converts"—clients who come to us after changing tutors at the end of spring testing because they "want a different perspective."

And that's not all: parents often wonder whether they should hire multiple tutors for different subject areas, whether it's best to choose a tutor based on geographic convenience or absolute expertise (in other words, the "online tutoring question"), and how much they really need to spend, in addition to a plethora of further questions. In truth, this part of the process can feel nearly as overwhelming for parents as does the actual preparation for students. I include two student stories below, which I hope will give you the insight needed to make your own informed decision.

Amy: Salt Lake City, 2017

Amy came late to the process—the beginning of August before her senior year. She possessed a ton of talent. A straight-A student in love with Math and Science, Amy ranked at the top of her class and demonstrated tremendous leadership in her community, particularly in the area of equal rights and professional mobility for young women. Despite her talent and success, Amy was stuck on a 29/30 composite on the ACT. She had done well on the second half of the ACT on her first sitting, and well on the first half of the ACT on her second sitting. She just needed to put it all together on one day—had she done so, she would have been at a 32 composite. Complicating her case, however, were psycho-physiological issues: the anxiety of the exam complicated preexisting stomach issues, which caused her intense pain and cramps during the exam.

Amy had been working with a local tutor in Salt Lake. The family did feel that the local tutor had provided Amy with good guidance, but Amy and her parents thought that a different perspective and approach might prove helpful. Although it was already late summer, Amy still had three more chances to take the ACT (September, October, and December) before she had to apply. While time was tight, she was all in and more than willing to do the work. As I told the family, ample time remained to help her reach her goals and position herself for admission to a terrific university well-matched to her ability and personal goals.

When she and I reviewed her diagnostic test, I noticed Amy's first obstacle: she simply did not believe that she could score a 32. In fact, I flat-out asked her: "Do you even believe that you *can* score a 33 or 34?" After a long pause, Amy sheepishly replied, "No." After some discussion, I realized that Amy possessed a healthy amount of "testing baggage" based on previously ingrained narratives: "I'm just not a good test-taker." Given that she had attended the same school since childhood and had never really needed to take high-stakes standardized tests, I kindly told her that her self-perception was, plainly, "BS." She was not a "Bad Test-Taker"—she was simply a novice.

To turn her in the right direction, I told her: "I literally *do not care* what may have happened in the past. You likely have not approached testing in the way that we're going to, so do yourself a favor and give yourself a clean slate—just as I am going to give you."

Once Amy began the process and we got to the heart of her mistakes, I realized her second issue: she wasn't aiming high enough. It became clear that Amy was someone who could score a 33 (guaranteed) and really a 34 if she played to win and remained consistent throughout the exam. But while Amy began to break into the mid- to high-30s in her practice, she remained inconsistent. Ultimately, the reason become clear: Amy had continued to work with the local tutor while simultaneously beginning to work with me. When the truth came out, Amy and her parents explained that "we thought the local, in-person support would give her added practice and further boost her confidence." Given Amy's situation and history, I certainly wanted remain open to any solution that might help her succeed. However, Amy's inconsistency stemmed from one of the primary reasons I do not recommend more than one tutor for ACT/SAT prep: she received competing advice. As a result, despite flashes of significant score improvements, as well as increased confidence and self-belief, Amy found it difficult to develop fluidity in her approach, causing yet more frustration for a kid who didn't need another iota.

Ultimately, we agreed on a strategy for how best to balance the guidance Amy received from the local tutor and from our sessions, but I'll admit that it entailed her committing to the path she and I had started down. To her credit, and to that of the local tutor who certainly played an important part in the process, Amy earned 32 on her September ACT and then 33 on the December ACT. She had risen to the occasion and finally scored in line with her potential—good enough to have helped her earn admission to a top five university. Furthermore, Amy had developed a deeper sense of personal confidence and rewritten the narrative around her status as "Bad Test-Taker," now qualifying as a "Bad-*Ass* Test-Taker."

While Amy's story illustrates the need to work within a coherent system, consistency within that system also promotes efficacy. Some students want (and some professionals advise) to work with one tutor on the Math side of the test and a different tutor for the Verbal side of the test. I can see the value in this: you want to work with an expert who is insanely good at what they do and absorb as much of their genius as you can. That makes perfect sense.

When it comes to standardized test preparation, though, I feel that it makes more sense to work with someone who can really teach you the entire test. There are obvious practical reasons for doing so (it's easier to schedule with one tutor than two, for instance), but I want to stress the strategic reasons for doing so.

First, one person is taking the test: you. While, yes, you do have (at least) two sides to your brain, it's in one head, and preparing under the guidance of one person helps you understand how to manage both sides of the brain during the test. This involves understanding how to manage your thoughts, emotions, and other abstract faculties during the testing experience. Working with more than one person on a single test might make sense if the experience were solely about the material—but, as we have already laid out, the test content itself represents only one-third of the challenge. Working with a single tutor allows you to hear input from one source that has analyzed information on your growth across all aspects of the test.

Second, working with one person provides you with a strategic advantage. Your tutor brings a multi-disciplinary skill set to your prep—this can prove incredibly helpful, especially when your tutor sees an opportunity to apply a tactic from one domain of the test towards another.

John: London, 2011

As an example, let's take John, a student from London whom I had the pleasure of tutoring a few years ago. Before his last test, John found himself struggling specifically with tone questions on the SAT. It was the one question type that continuously gave him difficulty and we had yet to find a way for him to solve them consistently. On one of our last days together before his October test, we finished up some Math, where he had done brilliantly. We had recently applied a new technique ("circle the details") to help him catch and correct careless errors. His score had increased quite dramatically as a result. After our break, we began to work on short paired reading passages (this was the Old SAT) and came upon a question regarding tone. It occurred to me that if John applied our "circle the details" tactic towards the language in the reading passages, particularly the verbs and adjectives, he would have a much stronger sense of the tone based on the author's choice in diction.

It worked. John successfully used this strategy—one that we had developed for the Math—on the Critical Reading, and his score improved greatly in both. To John, it felt like magic, and he was able to leverage this new momentum and achieve his target scores on the October test. This success can be directly drawn to the fact that John worked with one tutor on both sections. Had John been working with two different tutors on separate sections, there is a very low likelihood that John would have broken through on the Critical Reading and, ultimately, earned entry to his first-choice school—Georgetown.

Barriers to Success

Even the brightest students face barriers to succeeding on standardized tests. The unique and sophisticated nature of these exams can cause a variety of challenges, whether academic, psychological/emotional, physical, or spiritual. This section looks to explain these different barriers and provide strategies for mitigating their impact.

Academic

In short, academic barriers might be described as gaps between the school curriculum and material tested on the exam. These can vary widely for individual students and between different schools. However, students most often have difficulty in the following areas, all of which deserve special attention during preparation:

- Vocabulary
- Reading comprehension
- Writing skills
- Mathematic concepts

Certain groups of students may face additional academic barriers. International students, for instance, can face language barriers, not only in terms of the quantity of English words to which they have been exposed, but also in terms of meaning or connotation. For example, "conviction" proves to be a frequently misconstrued word. Most people, and virtually all that I have met outside the US, immediately think of conviction in a legal/criminal sense, as in "the prosecutor secured a conviction." Standardized tests (of course) anticipate this reality and often use "conviction" in its other sense: a firmly-held belief. Similar confusion sometimes occurs in the Math, where the familiar can become strange: students might read the word "slope" and feel utterly confused, for instance. Yet "slope" simply means "gradient," a basic concept that every international student with at least two years of high school math has seen multiple times and with which they probably feel quite familiar. Additionally, diagnosed or undiagnosed learning differences can impede students' progress across all testing areas. This is an excellent reason for families to speak with a licensed learning specialist if they feel that a student's progress is not where it could be—due to difficulties more fundamental than simply needing more practice or better instruction.

Most important to remember is that none of these challenges is insurmountable. Knowing precisely where your knowledge falls short is a crucial first step in planning your preparation for a successful test result. Mock tests are a great way to identify these weak spots, especially as they evolve and reappear.

Bear in mind that overcoming a weaker area might be an ongoing process for you. If every time you take a test it seems that you do better in one section and worse in another, you probably need to improve your consistency in preparation. Just because you made gains in an area does not mean that you can drop it from your prep schedule. You need to keep working at it—even if you have made breakthroughs and found success.

Physical

Physical factors play a significant role in determining performance. High schoolers have to deal with a variety of academic and social demands, and without proper self-care, they can easily fall victim to exhaustion and burnout. Specifically in regard to testing, students may allow their physical and emotional state to inform their choice of an answer. Be it in practice or in the heat of the test, students can sometimes choose the answer choice with which they feel an emotional connection in that moment. If you're regularly exhausted, no matter how well you've been coached or how many times you've done it correctly in the past, you will still struggle to succeed. I've seen many a student, drained, head down on the table, fall victim to "negative tone" answer choices because they were projecting their internal state rather than answering the question actually printed on the page or presented on the screen.

Exercise

One remedy for managing this physical/emotional connection is exercise, which can improve both mood and focus. One of our students in New Jersey recently credited her ACT score of 35 to a 2-week, 2-mile-run exercise regimen. Find what works for you, and take the time to implement an exercise plan. Try exercising regularly for the amount of time you need to stay focused. For example, if you need help with the Reading or Science section on the ACT, take brisk walks or jog for 35 minutes at a time to help condition your brain—and body—for that period of time. A number of studies have demonstrated that students who are more consistently active physically perform better on tests—especially in terms of mathematics and reading skills.[1]

Testing Environment

Another important, but sometimes overlooked, factor is the physical testing environment. Do you prefer to be seated at the front or the back of a room? In a small space or surrounded by other test-takers? Students should consider what is likely to work best for them and seek a testing center where their needs can be accommodated. This being said, students should also be prepared to manage and adapt to the environment if they find themselves in less than ideal circumstances—not an

---

1. For example, see:
    - Álvarez-Bueno, C. et al. "Academic Achievement and Physical Activity: A Meta-analysis." *Pediatrics*, vol. 140, no. 6, 2017.
    - Correa-Burrows, P. et al. "Physically active Chilean school kids perform better in language and mathematics." *Health Promotion International*, vol. 32, no. 2, 2014.

unlikely occurrence. In a nutshell, students, know and seek out what works best for you, but also build your resiliency, as we can never be in full control of our surroundings, whether in the test or elsewhere.

Psychological, Attentional, and Emotional

Despite the focus of most conventional thinking about test prep programs being on the test content and strategy (or "tricks," as some skeptics might say), in my experience, helping students to handle their psychological, attentional, and emotional barriers to success easily pays the largest dividends in terms of score improvement. By this, I mean teaching students to effectively cope with external distraction and, perhaps even more importantly, internal resistance. Actively thinking about and developing these skills proves crucial for test-takers, because our emotions and wider frame of mind together act as a gatekeeper for learning and performance. Only when we understand how to manage the nuances of our individual psychologies, and develop the self-discipline to do so consistently, can we make lasting improvements to the quality of our focus and, in turn, the results we produce.

Managing External Distraction

Time

Treat your test prep like an advanced level class. That means having dedicated weekly prep sessions, at a regularly scheduled time (and location), of no less than 30 minutes and no more than four hours. You should also plan for practice tests or mock tests on some select weekends. Some students look to do their test prep work in and directly after school (taking the late bus home, perhaps) and/or when they arrive home before they start their school homework. All that really matters is that you dedicate a time and stick to it. No excuses.

Space

Try to study in a calm, quiet environment where you're unlikely to be disturbed. This might be a school or public library, your bedroom, an empty classroom, or somewhere else. Whatever the case, take some time to organize your study space to create a clean and distraction-free zone.

"Turn off" so you can "turn on"

Although digital devices can be great tools for test prep, they can be even greater distractions when misused. Before you begin your session, eliminate potential digital diversions so you can apply undivided attention to your preparation. Turn off your phone. Turn notifications off on your computer. Close all tabs on your browser that are not relevant to your testing work. Mute sound on your computer (unless you're watching videos related to your test prep work, of course).

Other people

Advise your parents or guardians of your test prep schedule in advance. This way, they won't have to worry where you are if you stay late at school and, even more importantly, they'll know not to bother you while you study. It's probably best not to extend the same courtesy to your friends, however—no matter how many compassionate 'likes' you might pick up from a "stuck in the library" Instagram post, it's not going to help your performance and might well drain your focus from the task at hand.

Managing Internal Resistance

Show up prepared

Achieving focus can be tricky in the best of circumstances. Don't make it any harder by failing to show up ready for your test prep sessions. Have your work printed, papers organized, computer charged, and pencil case fully stocked. Remember to bring any necessary equipment, such as a graphing calculator (and batteries). Ensure you have a stable internet connection if needed for online prep. Last but certainly not least, arrive at your sessions with an agenda (containing three goals or fewer) for what you want to get done in the amount of time that you have.

Get it done—the right way

First and foremost, you have to complete the prep work you schedule—no excuses. But that is not all: when you're preparing, you should work as if you were in a test. A favorite coach of mine once told me that the secret to his success as a player was that he "practiced the practice" (i.e. he practiced "practicing" before the actual daily practice with his teammates) and he always "practiced as if [he was] actually playing the game." The numbers (hours, tests, etc.) quoted in this book mean *nothing* if those steps are not of the highest quality, meaning you must give nothing less than your absolute best in these times.

Overcome the fear of failure—and transcend the fear of success

Any number of thought patterns can cause internal resistance that impedes students' progress in preparation. For different students, this might be a fear of success ("I don't want to go to Chicago,"), a fear of failure ("What if I don't get in?"), or even both. Students have to face this internal resistance head on. You're in the arena. This is your shot. *Compete*. Every day you show up on time, do your absolute best to stay focused, and complete sessions strongly, you add 10 or more points to your score. Time to turn pro.

Outside factors like competition and peer pressure can also create internal resistance. Although a healthy competitive spirit can provide excellent motivation, students should generally avoid comparing themselves with their peers. As in life, there will nearly always be someone who seems smarter or better qualified. Students should make a conscious effort to take pride in their own achievements and to measure their success based on internal goals and aspirations. Conversely, high-achieving students should not feel compelled to limit themselves for fear of standing out from their social group.

Your real competition

You need to get over the comparison with your sister, brother, best friend, kid-in-the-front-of-class, mother, father, aunt, uncle, etc. Perhaps you feel threatened because you secretly believe that things come easier for them. Maybe you nosedive whenever you hear about their success and feel that they progressing more quickly than you. If this sounds at all like you, hear this: the only person you should compare yourself to is your ideal self. If you work harder—and smarter—than you ever have before, you'll find that eventually you *can* perform to your potential, and you'll surpass your current circumscribed sense of self because of it. But you must refocus yourself on what really matters and what's really going to produce results. Good news: if you are reading this book, you are already on your way. You just need to put your head down and get the job done in the time that you have left. Believe it: the more you do to condition yourself to perform to task, the more your attitude and behavioral habits will improve, and the higher your score will be.

Circling back to where this book started, in these moments, you need to remember who you want to be. Maybe you're scared of success because it means you're going to have to change, and the comfortable world you live in is going to vanish. You know what? It probably will. And you know what? Thank goodness. Because what will appear in its place is a different world, one that's much, much better—because you'll be honoring your true self and living the life that you truly yearn to experience. As that person, people will respect you and, more importantly, you will respect yourself. This is an opportunity for you to take control of your future, perhaps even to rewrite it. It will take time. It will take energy. It will take resilience. But it will happen. And rest assured—people will help you. Opportunities to speed your success will appear. And if you jump in, you will succeed, and you will look back on this journey as one of the formative experiences of your life. I promise.

Spiritual

I believe that there exists a 'spiritual' factor in successful testing. When a student possesses a strong sense of self, of their ambitions, and of faith in the possibilities of life and their talents, testing confidence grows far more easily. Students who lack a strong sense of their identity—and of their potential impact on or contribution to the world—can struggle to improve because they are unable to envision what they are working towards. It can be harder to find answers to these students' challenges, because their obstacles run deeper than envisioning their future or simply learning trigonometry. These students need to ask the right questions of themselves. A mentor, advisor, teacher, parent, friend, or even religious guide can help sort through these potentially difficult issues.

As already noted, successful testing requires adopting a certain mindset. For the purposes of the test, students have to believe that the universe sends us what we need when we need it—and that it rewards us for achievements when we truly earn them. I like to pass this thinking on to students during preparation, letting them know that the "testing gods" are watching over and rooting for them. There's certainly a level of faith and belief that students must possess when it comes to preparation (and, yes, it may need to develop over time). But as I remind every student who takes the process seriously: no one has ever worked as hard and as well as I'm asking you to work and not eventually earned their scores. Yes, it might take a test or two longer than we wish, but the universe rarely allows diligent, conscientious people to work that hard for that long without ultimately recognizing their efforts.

Step Zero

From a more practical standpoint, students should be able to think critically about their own performance and ask themselves some potentially tough questions. Have you really tried—or committed to—the approach your tutor or study plan is suggesting? Too many students don't fully embrace the preparation process—or, as I like to say, they have not completed "Step Zero"—and, in doing so, they reduce their chance of reaching their full potential. So ask yourself: have you really bought into the advice you've been given? Are you giving this your absolute best effort? Truly? Ask yourself!

Parenting Cues

Who's the most important player in the test prep and college admissions process? Parents. Why? Because they are there every moment between school, study, and tutoring sessions. Although all of the barriers described above can influence students' scores, parents can help to mitigate their effect. As a parent, there's a lot you can do to help your child deal with the pressures of testing and admissions, and you're also able to reinforce what advisors, counselors, and tutors have said or done. In short, parents are the glue in this process: you help to keep everything together—or not.

Evaluate how you handle stress

Each of us possesses conditioned responses to challenges and problems. Kids are perceptive, and they pick up on cues from parents—consequently, how you handle stress is likely how your daughter or son handles stress. If your kid is reacting adversely to the exam experience or preparation process, they might be mirroring what you have demonstrated to them, however unconsciously. Share the way you overcome stress with your kid. You are probably an expert on how to handle your emotions by now—pass along this wisdom to your child.

Set boundaries for talking about testing and admissions

Many students tire of constant conversation about testing and college applications. It's natural for parents to feel deeply invested in their kid's success, and it's certainly a good idea to help students stay on top of admissions timelines. From the student's perspective, though, there is a fine line between parental investment and nagging (!). Incessant testing and admissions talk can eat away at the student's patience and desire to do well on the test. Keep these conversations to 30 minutes per week once junior year comes around (perhaps 30 minutes twice per week during the second semester, if necessary). During senior year, consider building in a 15–30 minute window after dinner three or four times a week, or establish a 90–120 minute "college meeting" once a week to connect and complete action items.

Recognize hard work and get involved

Focus on positives during the preparation process—an important part of your role as a parent is being your kid's cheerleader. If a test comes back and scores have stagnated in Math but improved in English, devote your time to praising the hard work that went into the English score, not questioning what went wrong in Math. Relatedly, students need to know that their parents are there for them and ready to help out with this crucial, even formative, process. If your child doesn't want help right now, let them know that you respect their independence, are confident in their ability, and are there for support if ever needed.

- Furthermore, remember that defining progress can happen in many different ways throughout this journey. Some legitimate example of progress include:
- A good section that a student did timed or untimed for homework, which can indicate true potential
- A sub-section demonstrating a solid understanding of recently-learned techniques, even if hidden in a mock test with disappointing composite scores. The student may not have applied those techniques consistently throughout the test, but it's a start and can prove the springboard upon which to build a great deal of positive momentum
- Simply showing up for a mock test—particularly for students who were initially very resistant to the idea or reluctant to take test prep seriously and make it a part of their daily routine
- Taking a first exam with confidence and a feeling of preparedness

Diffuse social pressure

Make sure your kid understands that their capabilities are separate from those in their social group. Treat them like the great test-taker you want them to be. Let them know that they can succeed and that you're going to help them get the tools to do so.

Let kids take charge

Empower your child to be self-reliant, and let them know you believe in them. Emotions such as fear and anxiety are totally normal and controllable. Allow your child the room to manage their personal obstacles independently, knowing that you can step in at any time, if necessary. One of the best, but perhaps most daunting, things about the testing process is that, for some students, it's one of the first challenges that they need to tackle all on their own: Mom and Dad cannot do it for them. While this may challenge students at first, it's ultimately an opportunity to transition to adulthood.

Pinpoint fears

Ask questions. Discuss different outcomes and how you will respond to them. What are they afraid of? Disappointing you? Living up to an older sibling? Retaking the test? Discuss what happens when failure occurs and when success occurs. Remind your kid that you will love them no matter what.

Encourage them to no end

Always, always, always encourage your kid to think positively, and celebrate their success and effort throughout the journey. Reward small goals. Testing is a win-win. Nobody fails. Successful people have gone to all sorts of different schools. Let them know you're proud of what they have done—not what they score. Build confidence every day: it will pay off once the test comes around.

Know your limits

Parents are crucial in the testing and admissions process, but it's important to know when to step back. This is where *you* must exercise self-discipline. Some kids—many kids, in fact—will need an expert's help to achieve their potential. This isn't a weakness, either on your part or your child's, and you shouldn't hesitate to find your kid external help if they need it. The types of support students need will vary widely: some might need a tutor, others might benefit from talking with a therapist, and others still might require intervention from a licensed learning specialist. What you can do is be attentive to your kid's progress and be open to the possibility of finding the external support your child might need to achieve—and extend—their full potential.

Conclusion

Your Roadmap

Make no mistake: success leaves tracks. The students who succeed on their tests have been thinking about them for months, if not years, and they have devised a step-by-step plan for achieving their target scores. They have envisioned their ideal self, what they want to do, and the impact the wish to make on the world. They have allowed this vision to guide every action taken on the path to test day, graduation, and beyond.

To help you create your own preparation plan, I've produced a 50-Step Test Prep Roadmap for you to fill out and return to as your testing journey progresses. The Roadmap—of which there are two versions, customized for the SAT and ACT—is designed to help you stay on schedule with a step-by-step plan for your preparation process, while ensuring you cover all the essential bases of content, strategy, and test-taking skill. You'll benefit from careful guidance on which topics to focus on, when to begin, and how long each element should take. All of which leaves more time for you to focus on the prep itself—and, thus, building towards the scores you need to become the successful person you want to be. To download the Roadmap and get started, type the link into your web browser:

https://catestutoring.com/GE-Roadmap

The Guarantee

I am not exaggerating when I describe this process as a "guarantee" for SAT/ACT success. But it is up to you to ensure this guarantee. Doing so rests solely upon your preparation.

New York, 2002

Let me provide an example. In 2002, I tutored two different students for the Biology SAT Subject test. Both students were intelligent and interesting, and both had the capacity to score very well on the test. Student A, who was probably the more academically inclined of the two, scored a 560 on the diagnostic, while Student B scored a 540. After tutoring both students for a number of weeks in preparation for the exam, I noticed that their respective work habits and levels of discipline were quite different. Student A—who knew he was smart—normally did not complete the assigned homework, instead using our sessions as his time to study. Student B, however, dedicated consistent time and energy to her prep between sessions and used our time together to ask very specific questions on the material, practice questions she could not figure out on her own, and learn more generally about the ins-and-outs of the test. These two students took the same test on the same day, prepared with the same tutor, and were given the same set of assignments. When the test date arrived, both felt prepared to score well. When their scores came back, Student A scored a 620—a modest improvement. Student B, however, scored a 740. What was the difference? Student B put in a concerted effort to increase her score, while Student A took a more casual approach and relied on his existing abilities. While 620 is a nice score, Student A knew that he was capable of scoring just as well as Student B did—if not even higher. Unfortunately, he didn't.

The stories of Students A and B are illustrative of so many others I have encountered during my 15+ years in test prep. More so than preexisting "ability," educational background, or any other factor, commitment and self-discipline decide scores. Student B exercised these valuable personal traits, while Student A did not.

Question is: which student are you?

The choice is yours. Start thinking about and planning your test preparation process now, and make sure you stick to your plan. That's really all it takes. Remember, all of the skills required by standardized tests are learnable. I repeat: all of these skills are learnable. The only difference between you and me when it comes to standardized test-taking is that I have seen more questions. That's it. Truly. Did you learn how to ride a bike? Can you swim? Learning how best to test is no different. You already know most of this material. The challenge is simply learning—and practicing—how to apply it on test day.

Parents, the way to ensure that your child has the scores they need for admission to their top choice school is to help them understand how they need to think about the test. That's where it starts. This is not school. This is athletic training, and the greatest challenges involved in the process relate to the mental aspects (focus, endurance, commitment) much more so than the academic aspects. At its core, standardized testing is truly about mastery over one's self, or in other words:

CONCLUSION

self-discipline. Once you and your child commit to this truth, your family's success will become inevitable. Guaranteed.

Good luck!

Appendix

Overview of Tests

In general, standardized tests are intended to provide high schools and colleges with an objective gauge by which to compare students of similar academic record and from differing educational systems and curriculums.

The ISEE and SSAT, which are created by and administered by the Educational Records Bureau (ERB), provide a measure by which to gauge a student's academic skill development up through early 8th grade. The SAT—which, along with the PSAT and SAT Subject Tests, is created by Educational Testing Service (ETS) and administered by the College Board—is meant to give colleges a sense of how well a student may perform in their first year in college. SAT Subject Tests offer colleges information on how well a student's school course has prepared them in comparison to another student who took the same course at a different school. The American College Test (ACT) plays a similar role in the admissions process as the SAT.

How the Tests Work

The following list highlights the main features of the tests students might encounter on the road to college acceptance:

- **ISEE:** tests all areas of math as well as reading comprehension and vocabulary, which can prove a challenge
- **SSAT:** tests many domains, much like the ISEE, but vocab questions offer little context and are usually more difficult
- **PSAT:** a preliminary SAT; students who score in the top 1% of test-takers in their state may qualify as a National Merit Scholar
- **SAT:** a general reasoning test; test-makers study the material students learn in school and then tweak its representation on the test
- **SAT Subject Tests:** more content-based than the SAT; however, students can still struggle to reach their full potential due to a lack of proper test-specific strategy
- **ACT:** a popular alternative to the SAT, the ACT also features a science section and can be a better fit for students with strong verbal skills

Keys to Successful Test Prep

If you've already read this book, you won't find much new information here, but for newcomers, here's a high-level summary of the considerations successful test-takers will bear in mind:

- **Fit:** choose the test (SAT, ACT, Math I vs. Math II Subject Test, etc.) best suited to strengths
- **Timing:** schedule and sit tests at the most opportune time for success

- **Personalization:** develop and internalize strategies specific to their individual skill set
- **Mock Tests:** consistently schedule and sit mock tests; the more mock tests, the higher the score
- **Third Time's the Charm:** take the ISEE/SSAT/SAT/ACT at least twice, or as many as three times

SAT vs. ACT Guide

If you are a sophomore or rising junior, one of the biggest questions you face on the road to admission at a US college is which test to take: SAT or ACT? Your decision carries great importance. Ultimately, it may be a deciding factor in which schools make your final list, as the most selective colleges seek students with not only excellent academic and extracurricular records, but also strong test scores.

Most testing agencies suggest that you take a diagnostic exam to identify which test is likely to suit you better. This is good advice, as trying out each exam provides you with a first-hand, personal taste of what the SAT and ACT each offer. However, many students do not have access to expert feedback on which exam suits them better after taking these diagnostic tests, which can make the decision a hard one to make.

Strengths-Based Decision Making

One way to decide which test is a better fit involves taking one's academic strengths into consideration. For example, students strong in reading comprehension may consider the ACT, as the ACT essentially rewards strong reading comprehension skills across the entire exam, even in the Math and

Science tests. Similarly, a student strong in math (who might, in turn, be comparatively weaker in reading comprehension) may consider the SAT, which tests higher-level math skills.

SAT vs. ACT: Strengths-Based Decision Table				
If you are great at...	**English**	**Math**	**Reading**	**Science**
Then take the...	ACT	SAT	ACT	SAT

You might be thinking, "Wait a second. If I am strong at science, you recommend that I take the SAT? Wouldn't it be smarter for me to take the ACT? It has a science section, and science is a strength for me." Maybe. However, the Science test on the ACT does not *really* test science. Frankly, it tests comprehension skills. A background in science, while admittedly helpful, is not necessary for a high score on the Science test, or even a perfect score. Furthermore, students who lean more towards the sciences may not have as strongly-developed skills in English and reading comprehension. As a result, even if the student does, in fact, do well on the ACT Science test, the ACT English and Reading tests might prove to be a great challenge. The idea that science students should take the ACT because it has a Science section might be the single most erroneous assumption made by students deciding between the SAT and ACT.

Weaknesses-Based Decision Making

At CATES, we strive to focus on the positive at all times. That said, sometimes the SAT vs. ACT decision will come down to working around a shortcoming or weakness in your skills. For example, students who do not pursue advanced math courses tend to favor the ACT because the math tested on the exam aligns well with fundamental math curricula. By contrast, the SAT Math, after the redesign, resembles the Math Level II SAT Subject Test material (which is more advanced than ACT Math) and also includes a No Calculator section. For these reasons, students who are weaker in math should probably consider the ACT, which tests more familiar concepts and allows the use of a calculator throughout the entire Math test.

SAT vs. ACT: Weaknesses-Based Decision Table				
If you are not great at...	English	Math	Reading	Science
Then take the...	SAT	ACT	SAT	ACT

Circumstances-Based Decision Making

For some students, the decision to take the SAT or ACT comes down to personal circumstances beyond their academic strengths and weaknesses. Students who struggle with time, for instance, often favor the SAT over the ACT, because the SAT provides students with more time for fewer questions. This is especially true in the Evidence-Based Reading section of the SAT compared to the ACT Reading section. Mastering the timing on the Math, Reading, and Science sections is a critical component to success on the ACT. For some students, this can be a difficult skill to develop, especially without consistent, dedicated practice.

Students who have a limited budget might consider the ACT for a few reasons. First, many schools waive their SAT Subject Test requirements for students who opt for the ACT with Writing. Schools such as Brown, Rice, Tufts, and Wellesley fall into this category. Be aware, however, that some schools, such as CalTech, Carnegie Mellon, and Cornell, still require SAT Subject Tests, regardless of whether you opt for the ACT with Writing. Students should research the testing requirements for each college to which they intend to apply.

Students who arrive late to the process should think about taking the ACT. More than anything, this is to make scheduling easier. The ACT is administered in early September and again in late October. The SAT is administered in early October and early November.

While both ACT and SAT students have two shots at the exam before the 1 November Early Decision/Action deadline, ACT-takers can receive their first scores before the end of September, allowing them a full month to adjust in their preparation before they resit the ACT in October. SAT-takers receive their scores near the end of October and then have only a week for adjustments. If you're banking on hitting your SAT targets on the October exam but discover a week before your November Subject Tests that your SAT score isn't strong enough for your Early Decision/Action School, it's probably too late to change.

Still unsure of which test to take?

Finally, the simple answer to the SAT vs. ACT question is this: take the test on which you will score higher. Seems obvious, right? Not so much.

Often, a student may take a diagnostic SAT or ACT and score better on one test, but ultimately decide to take the other. Why? Sometimes the test on which you initially score higher is not the test on which you could improve the most over time. A good number of students, for example, initially score higher on the ACT, but, in fact, show more long-term promise on the SAT. For instance, a student may learn how to really attack a section of weakness (the Math, for instance) such that it raises their SAT score to a level that overtakes their maximum ACT score. At CATES, we created an SAT vs. ACT diagnostic test specifically to diagnose this phenomenon. Review your SAT vs. ACT diagnostics with an expert to identify your target scores on each test. You may be surprised by what you learn.

SAT Subject Tests

SAT Subject Tests act as a supplement to the SAT or ACT and demonstrate your knowledge in a specific domain. Taking two SAT Subject Tests is required by several top-tier schools, but at the majority of schools they are optional or can be waived by taking the ACT + Writing. It's common for STEM programs to require applicants to take the Math II and Physics Subject Tests.

Below is the full list of available SAT Subject Tests:

- Literature

- *History:*
  - US History
  - World History
- *Math:*
  - Math Level 1
  - Math Level 2
- *Science:*
  - Biology
  - Chemistry
  - Physics
- *Foreign Languages:*
  - Chinese with Listening
  - French
  - French with Listening
  - German
  - German with Listening
  - Italian
  - Japanese with Listening
  - Korean with Listening
  - Latin
  - Modern Hebrew
  - Spanish
  - Spanish with Listening

If your colleges of choice require you to take SAT Subject Tests, start thinking now about which tests will provide you with the best opportunity to demonstrate your expertise. Then, read on for the insider tips that will help you score at your very best.

Content

SAT Subject Tests are much more straightforward than the SAT or ACT because they are more content-based. If you know the content, you should do well. In that respect, the Subject Tests become fairly simple to prepare for.

Keys To Content Review Success

At some point, the student will have reviewed all the relevant concepts on the test and the balance of the prep schedule will be about mock tests and further reinforcement of the material. During this time, it may be smart for the student to complete two practice tests a week from a variety of prep books—in addition to mock tests on weekends—so that they can see the information presented in different contexts. 80% of the exam—real and practice—is about factual recall. That other 20%—the differentiator between 670 and 720, for example—is about application of that knowledge. None of the books on the market provide application of knowledge questions as strong or sophisticated as the real exam, but by doing multiple tests from multiple providers, students will develop some sense of taking their understanding of a topic in one light and applying it in another. If the student does enough practice tests, she will feel more confident on test day.

Strategy

Below, I've included some top strategy tips for the Subject Tests. If you have already read the Strategy Essentials section from Chapter 4, you might notice a striking similarity between the advice I gave there and what is presented here: that's because, for the most part, *it is the same advice!* This speaks to the idea of "compound interest" in test preparation that I mentioned earlier: because so many of the skills and strategies required by one standardized test cross-apply to other tests, preparation for one often becomes preparation for another, without any extra work on your part. Now that's what I call a return on investment.

For Questions:

Circle & Associate

In general, "Circle & Associate" is by far the most helpful technique on Subject Tests. Circle & Associate recommends that the student circle the details (facts) in each question and then ask: "what are the first three things that come to mind when I see that?" Normally, the ideas the student associates with those facts lead the student to the correct answer, be it directly or indirectly. If nothing else, C&A helps students isolate the important facts in the question so that they are thinking clearly about the given information.

Some students may prefer to underline the details in the question rather than circle the details. Don't do it! Underlining may help a student as they read the material for the first time, but it fails to differentiate the important details from the less important information upon review. Circling the details highlights the critical information more effectively, and allows the student to work more efficiently.

For Answer Choices:

Get Rid Of What You Know Is Wrong, And Choose The Best Of What's Left

Like the SAT and the ACT, the Subject Tests aren't always about finding the "right" answer, but rather about finding the "best" answer. There are questions where we do not know why Choice C, for example, is correct, other than the fact that we know that Choices A, B, D, and E are wrong for any one of the following reasons:

- **Too Extreme:** the answer choices contain strong words, such as: always, never, deeply, strongly, etc.
- **Half Right:** the first half of the question contains information that is correct for the question, but the second half of the answer does not, or vice-versa
- **True But Wrong:** the answer choice is a statement that is true for the subject, but wrong for the question being asked.
- **Off-Topic/Out-of-Context:** the information in the answer choice is completely irrelevant to the question at hand, or even simply false.

Often, it's easier—and quicker—to look for what is wrong with an answer choice, find it, and eliminate it, rather than look for why an answer choice may or may not be right. This can feel like a big adjustment for the test-taker, but it's an adjustment that may be necessary in order to be more successful on the exam.

Degree of Difficulty

For the most part, the material on the Subject Tests gets harder as you progress through the test. For Subject Tests that feature different sections (A, B, & C, for example on the Science or Foreign Language tests), the degree of difficulty reboots once you move into the next section. For example, the Chemistry Subject Tests features three distinct sections: A) Multiple-Answer Questions; B) "Correct Explanations"; and C) Standard Multiple Choice. Each section has its own self-contained set of Easy, Medium, and Hard questions. Question 25 in Section A should seem a lot harder than Question 101 in Section B, which is the very next question on the test, and probably classified as an "easy" question.

Final Steps and "Usable Scores"

Unlike the SAT or ACT, students actually can cram for Subject Tests (but are not encouraged to!), due to their being more content-heavy than the general skills tests. To that point, if you are feeling nervous about the exam in the last week or two, the reality is that it mostly comes down to knowing the material. If you know all the material before you walk into the exam, you can score something in the mid-to-high 600s on most of the tests. Strategy and smart test-taking (knowing when to omit, how to guess, and practicing emotional/psychological control) can help you score into the 700s.

Once more, if students can simply memorize everything in the prep book's content review, they have a great chance to earn what we call a "usable" score, meaning it is strong enough to submit to most schools. You can calculate the "usability" of a Subject Test score by looking a school's average SAT composite score and dividing it by three. For the elite Ivy-caliber schools, such as Harvard, Yale, Princeton, MIT, and Stanford, with average SAT composites between 1500 and 1550 (out of 1600), you want Subject Test scores around 750 and above (figure no less than 720). For the next set of schools, such as Brown, Cornell, Georgetown, Wesleyan, etc., a usable score is 720 and above (no less than 700). For the next tier of schools, it's a 670. If you're shooting for a top-30 school, nothing less than 650 should be sent, and nothing below 600 should really be sent to any school in the top 50 (and perhaps not to any school at all).

What to Know About the Foreign Language Tests

Foreign language exams appear in two versions: Reading-only and Reading with Listening. The two versions are considered different tests, so you could take both and they would count as two separate SAT Subject Tests. That said, you're probably better served by demonstrating some range in your subjects, with a Humanities-based exam and a Math/Science-based exam, if you have the ability to do so.

The Listening versions of the exams are only given in November, and contain one section where the student listens to and answers questions about foreign-language dialogues. The Listening section usually counts for about 1/3 of the total score of the test. Students *must* register for Listening version tests before the registration deadline. Standby testers cannot take Listening tests.

Lastly—and this applies to bilingual students, international students, and those studying at, for example, a French, Italian, or Mandarin high school in the US—taking a foreign language test in your native tongue can be a double-edged sword. You will be expected to earn an elite score (in fact, probably 800), and if you do not, the admissions officers could hold it against you.

Case Studies

Adam

A talented baseball player from New York, Adam completed his diagnostic in February of 2016 (his sophomore year) with the following ACT scores:

- Composite: 20
- English: 18
- Math: 21
- Reading: 19
- Science: 20

Adam wanted to apply to schools such as Middlebury and University of Chicago (two very different schools, indeed) because they had very strong academic programs—particularly in economics and computer science (yes, Middlebury, a liberal arts college, possesses great math and science-oriented programs)—as well as highly competitive NCAA Division III baseball teams. He needed to hit a super score (that is, the highest test scores across all sittings recalculated to create a "super composite") of 32 or higher. Thus, based on his goals, Adam needed help all across the board, and a 12 point jump in his composite. To complicate matters further, Adam had a learning difference that strongly delayed his processing of language, particularly when it came to reading. As a result, he struggled with reading prompts longer than two or three lines and possessed incredible weaknesses in grammar and general comprehension that had affected him for years. Unsurprisingly, given these challenges, Adam's confidence in his ability to succeed on the ACT could have been stronger. And, given his ambitious goals, the task seemed tall—if not completely out of reach.

But we set about in earnest, taking care to modify our methods in order to accommodate Adam's schedule and needs. Since athletes need to have their testing complete by the end of junior year, for recruiting purposes, we set the October ACT as a soft target for Adam's first test. Additionally, Adam liked working online just as much as working in person, and given his baseball schedule, doing so allowed him the flexibility to keep his appointments while training and playing baseball across the New York City area. Moreover, it became clear early on that writing Adam's notes for him on a Google doc (most of the time, at least) was the most effective and efficient way to promote his progress. A visual learner, rather than a kinesthetic or aural one, Adam processed and understood the material best when he saw it appearing letter-by-letter before his eyes.

Adam's formal preparation began in the summer after his sophomore year. Bearing in mind Adam's strengths and weaknesses, for his first test we designed a program that initially focused heavily on learning English grammar. ACT English tests umpteen grammar rules, and its inner architecture is founded mostly on context. Another reason to focus carefully on grammar: the test is fond of providing tricky answer choices that appeal to the ear of a contemporary student, but wouldn't fly with your English professor. From there, we taught Adam all of the Math, which took some time due to the sheer volume of material but came relatively more quickly to Adam than the other sections due to his strength in Math. From there, we turned our attention to strategy on the Science and then tackled the Reading. Unfortunately, we could not address the Reading as completely as we had hoped before Adam's first test due to normal fluctuations in the preparation program (scheduling conflicts, student illness, school priorities, extenuating personal circumstances, etc.). Progress in general came slowly (which is fine), and Adam needed to delay his first actual test to December. His scores were as follows:

- Composite: 30 (+10)
- English: 33 (+15)
- Math: 31 (+10)
- Reading: 24 (+5)
- Science: 31 (+11)

Clearly, Adam made tremendous progress on his first test. Double-digit increases are incredibly impressive, especially on the composite score. However, we had more work to do, and so we focused next on boosting the non-English sections, particularly the Reading.

On his second test, in February, only six weeks after his December test, Adam scored the following:

- Composite: 31 (+11 points from diagnostic)
- English: 31 (+13 points)
- Math: 32 (+11 points)
- Reading: 31 (+12 points)
- Science: 32 (+12 points)

Although his English score dropped a couple of points, Adam made gains in each of the non-English sections, including an amazing additional seven points in the reading, bringing his total improvement to 12 points.

At this point, Adam and I had been meeting three days a week, on average, for roughly six months before his first test in December (60 hours) and then again for six weeks (18 hours) before his resit in February. In the process, Adam took six mock tests and his scores, when taken at their highest (as schools do), now stood at the following:

- Composite: 31 (32 Super Composite, +11-12 points)
- English: 33 (+15 points)
- Math: 31 (+10 points)
- Reading: 31 (+12 points)
- Science: 32 (+12 points)

Despite a number of personal and practical obstacles, then, Adam ended up with the scores he needed for entry to his top choice schools by February. And because he started early, Adam had the flexibility to either accept these already excellent scores and move on to other parts of the admissions process, or sit the test again to improve even further. Ultimately, he chose to resit the ACT in June to improve his Math to a 34 or higher and move his Super Composite closer to 33. He did—and then some:

- Composite: 34 (34 Super Composite, +14 points)
- English: 31 (+13 points)
- Math: 34 (+13 points)
- Reading: 34 (+15 points)
- Science: 35 (+15 points)

Clearly, Adam (to borrow a baseball term) "knocked it out of the park" on the June test, earning the composite and section scores that were in line with his true ability, which proved greater and greater over the course of the process. Furthermore, Adam's improvements (coupled with his athletic talent) opened more doors for him. When he applied, he self-reported the following scores on his Common Application:

- Composite: 34 (34 Super Composite, +14 points)
- English: 33 (+15 points)
- Math: 34 (+13 points)
- Reading: 34 (+15 points)
- Science: 35 (+15 points)

These scores allowed Adam to apply early decision to Johns Hopkins—arguably the most rigorous academic and athletic environment for baseball players, as a top-10 college with a top-10 baseball team—and he was accepted. Adam had found a terrific match both academically and athletically. How did he get there? He believed that improvement was possible and was willing to do the work—even alongside his school and baseball commitments (which took up virtually all of his time)—to get the scores he knew that he could earn.

Julie

Julie, a very bright student from London, came to CATES wanting to follow in the footsteps of her siblings, who already attended Yale and Georgetown, and study at an American college. Julie started out well, with the following ACT diagnostic scores, taken in June 2015:

- Composite: 25
- English: 22
- Math: 23
- Reading: 30
- Science: 25

Given this strong starting position, we set a target composite score of 34+, with no individual section to fall below 32. Despite her promising performance, however, Julie was very concerned that her "slowness" during tests would not allow her to improve much upon her Reading score and so might hinder her ability to meet the target.

Starting in the summer after Year 11 (that's sophomore year of high school, for American readers), we convened online twice a week for an hour (or a little more in the summer due to her extra free time), with in-person meetings in London or New York every 6–8 weeks. Our online meetings would employ a variety of platforms: we talked on Skype, used collaborative Google docs, and jointly analyzed scoring patterns via CATES

HQ (our proprietary online software), as well as keeping notes on paper.

By her first actual test, in October 2015, Julie had made excellent progress and produced the following scores:

- Composite: 31 (+6 points)
- English: 29 (+7 points)
- Math: 26 (+3 points)
- Reading: 36 (+6 points)
- Science: 33 (+8 points)

In our post-test debrief, Julie explained that she had succumbed to nerves at the start of the test, explaining her comparatively smaller improvement on the Math section, but to her credit she regained control at the break and did incredibly well on the second half of test. For Julie, this experience was a breakthrough in itself: she now understood—from first-hand experience—that it's possible to take full control over yourself, even in the high-stakes testing environment.

By December 2015, Julie had built further on this experience, earning the following test scores:

- Composite: 33 (+8 points)
- English: 35 (+13 points)
- Math: 31 (+8 points)
- Reading: 36 (+6 points)
- Science: 31 (+6 points)

By this point, Julie had almost achieved her target composite score. We honed in on her mistakes and determined that the main barrier to that final point was simply a tendency to let her focus lapse. Julie seemed to be struggling with complete commitment to the process, and so was experiencing frustration with herself.

The night before her real ACT test, we had the "the big" conversation: "the silly mistakes have got to *stop*." Julie already had the knowledge, the ability, and the skills. She had put the practice hours in. Now, she needed to embrace her absolute best and just get the job done. Self-discipline was the key. This was a coaching conversation—centered not on academics nor even on test strategy, but instead on challenging the student to honor this process, her effort, and the reality that she knew exactly what she had to do. She just needed to do it. And she did—when her final scores came in, we were both delighted with her tremendous success:

- Composite: 34 (+9 points)
- English: 35 (+13 points)
- Math: 32 (+9 points)
- Reading: 36 (+6 points)
- Science: 33 (+8 points)

Julie indeed achieved her ultimate testing goal as well as her overall college goal by earning admission to Duke, a top-ten American college. Her scores proved critical to her acceptance.

Franco

Franco, an exceptional student in the top 1% of his class at a British boarding school, came to CATES with a raft of accomplishments and qualifications: he was an international ski racer, with Olympic aspirations, and a nationally-recognized academic. With these great accomplishments came great ambition: Franco had his heart set on attending a top-three US college, and he thus needed no less than a 34 ACT composite score. His excellent July diagnostic test results suggested that this would be a more-than-achievable target:

- Composite: 31
- English: 26
- Math: 33
- Reading: 31
- Science: 33

Franco had a decided Type A personality, and he needed to control all aspects of his preparation routine to ensure success. For the most part, he led tutoring sessions, coming prepared with the knowledge of exactly what he needed and aiming to make use of tutoring sessions to gain valuable insight into the forces behind his mistakes and learn proven strategies for how to manage and eliminate them. He created his own preparation system, using Microsoft OneNote, that his CATES tutor was happy to work within so as to achieve the best likelihood of success. Franco met with his tutor for 30–60 minutes, twice a week on average, with the length and content of the sessions adapting entirely based on the student's evolving needs.

By October, this approach had begun to bear fruit, with the composite score on his first actual test already placing Franco close to his target:

- Composite: 32 (+1 points)
- English: 34 (+8 points)
- Math: 35 (+2 points)
- Reading: 32 (+1 point)
- Science: 27 (-6 points)

In truth, however, based on his strong diagnostic Franco ought to have exceeded these scores, even at this stage. A lack of mock tests in the lead up to the first exam prevented him from building the necessary endurance to stay consistently focused through the entire sitting. Thus, his science score fell six points from the diagnostic, dragging his composite down to a 32—a great score, to be sure, but Franco's growth in the program showed serious potential for him to earn a composite of 35 or 36.

By placing extra focus on mock tests in the run up to his April exam, we helped Franco to realize this potential:

- Composite: 35 (+4 points)
- English: 36 (+10 points)
- Math: 36 (+2 points)
- Reading: 31 (even)
- Science: 36 (+3 points)

Clearly, Franco did a tremendous job in this exam, building on his successful mock test regimen to position himself for perfect scores in three of the four sections, as well as the composite.

In looking at all both his ACT exams together, ie. super scoring, Franco, along with his perfect 800 in the Math Level II SAT Subject Test and 800 in the Latin SAT Subject Test, has clearly met the highest standards on the ACT for the very top US colleges:

- Composite: 35 (+4 points)
- English: 36 (+10 points)
- Math: 36 (+2 points)
- Reading: 32 (+1 point)
- Science: 36 (+3 points)

Adding to his nationally-recognized athletic and academic merits, these scores helped Franco to distinguish himself from the other students in his competitive applicant year. He was to his first-choice college, Harvard.

Expected Results: Revisited

After all this talk of prep progress and score increases, you might be recalling an earlier section of this book, "Expected Results," where I outlined the score improvements that can typically be expected by students starting out with different diagnostic scores. As luck would have it, Adam, Julie, and Franco more or less fall into the three buckets I outlined there, i.e. diagnostic scores of up to 20, up to 25, and up to 30. So how did these three compare with the "average" test-taker?

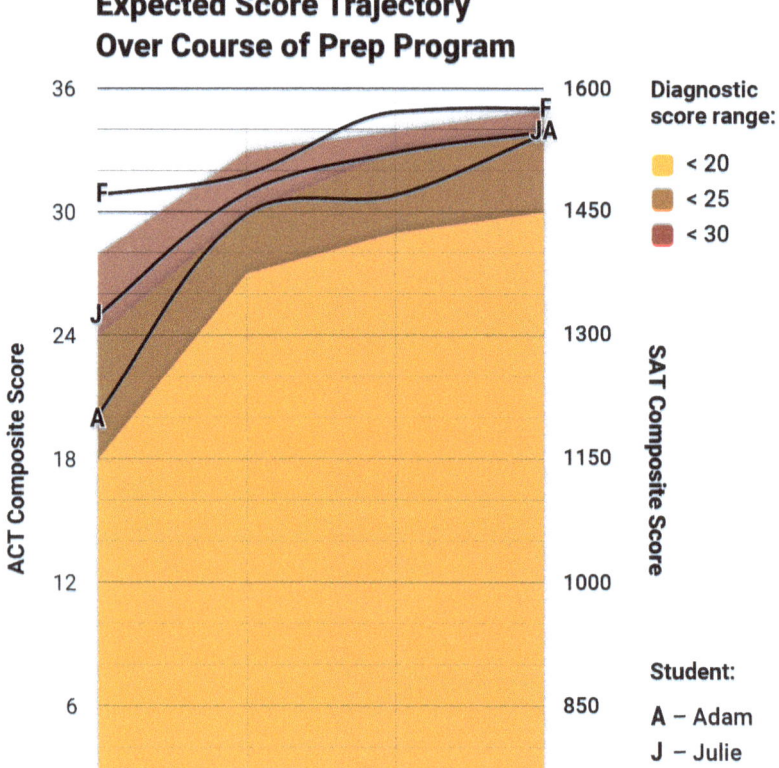

Starting out with a particularly high diagnostic score of 31, Franco ended up with a 35 composite—an excellent score that we would often expect from students with such strong starting profiles. Starting with a 25 and finishing with a 34, Julie also tracked the progress of the "average" test-taker with her starting scores fairly closely. The real standout of this story is Adam, who, despite starting the process with a 20, managed to smash through the score range we would typically expect for a student with his diagnostic. His case goes to show that no score prediction is set in stone. If you're passionate and truly committed—as Adam was—you *can* get the score you want, no matter where you begin.

Scoring FAQs

» How much is my score likely to fluctuate on test day?

At CATES, we've pretty much seen it all. A safe estimate on the ACT is probably +/- 2 points on each section and the composite. For the SAT and Subject Tests, students often see a fluctuation of +/- 30–50 points. It depends on how much work you do between sessions and how many mock tests you sit in a simulated testing environment. The students who score closest to or at their medians are the ones who take the most mock tests.

» Will universities see all the tests I take?

It depends on their Score Choice policy. For example, Georgetown requires that you submit all SAT and Subject Test scores. However, Harvard allows you to submit whatever scores you wish. This information can be found on the school website and on the College Board website. Regardless of the policy, all schools consider your highest scores. Thus, even if you are forced to send a low score to a school like Georgetown, if you retook that test and did better, Georgetown will evaluate your application on the basis of the higher score.

For the ACT, Score Choice exists for most schools. However, policies change all the time, and you should check out the school's website for further information.

» **I'm happy with my scores. Should I take the test again?**

If your scores are at the median or above the median range for a school, probably not. For example, at Yale the median ACT range is 31-35. If you scored 33 or above, you should be all set. The only caveat is if your mock test median was, for example, 35 and you scored a 33, which would suggest that you haven't yet realized your testing potential.

» **My scores are borderline. Should I take the test again?**

It depends on your school goals and mock test medians. If you were trending at, say, a 32 on the ACT but scored a 30 or 31, you might still be positioned well if a school's median range is 29–32. However, if the school's range is 29–32 and you scored a 28 or a 29, you should definitely consider taking it again.

Also keep in mind that, on the ACT, a 1–2 point drop from your mock test median composite is not uncommon. That's a 30–50 point decrease in SAT terms. In fact, this kind of fluctuation is expected on first tests. If you drop more than this amount from your mock test median composite, you should almost definitely take the test again. The only exception would be if your actual score was still above—or better yet well above—the average score for the school.

In regards to the SAT Subject Tests, to gauge how your scores match up against the school's standards, look at the school's average individual section scores (or the average SAT composite, divided by 2) and use that as your barometer. For example, at Trinity College, the average SAT composite is about a 1320. Thus, for Subject Tests you want your scores to be at 660 or above. If you are applying to Yale, which has an average SAT composite of 1540, your Subject Test scores want to be close to or above 770.

» What happens if I get deferred?

Applicants are deferred for many reasons. Test scores can play a part. If you do get deferred and feel you can do better on the exam, you should definitely consider taking it again.

» Can I withdraw my application for Early Decision/Action, so I can retest and apply during Regular?

It's possible. CATES has worked with students who have successfully requested that their application be moved from the Early Decision (binding commitment) or Early Action (non-binding commitment) applicant pool to the regular round, but these instances are unique. If you do wish to have your application pushed to the regular round, you will need to speak with the school to which you applied to see what options exist.

» Do I have to send the scores?

If you listed on your Common Application that you were taking the exam, then yes, the school will expect you to send the scores. If you did not list in the Common Application that you were taking the exam, then you can get away with not sending the scores. There is one exception, however. For schools that do not honor Score Choice, and thus require you to send them all scores, then you must send all your test results, no matter how pleased (or not) you are with them.

Myth & Reality for International Students

Many international students ask the same question: "Do colleges understand that I'm taking the [insert national diploma examination] and that we don't study the SAT/ACT in school? Do they take that into consideration when making their decision?" The question they're really asking is this: "Will [enter Elite College name here] give me some leniency when it comes to test scores because I take finals?" The answer is the same every time: no.

This wishful misconception arises from a few myths commonly held by international applicants to American colleges. Let's debunk them, one by one, before looking at the realities of testing for international students.

MYTH 1:
All American students prepare for the SAT/ACT in class

This myth is born from the belief that, as is the case in many other countries, the American education system has a final, cumulative set of examinations that cap off your secondary school education and lead you into college. The British A-level system works this way, and the International Baccalaureate falls into this category as well. The results of these exams are used almost exclusively as the criteria for college entrance.

America is different. Here, we take final examinations in our subjects at the end of each and every year and those four years of final grades are used as the criteria for admission. There are pros and cons for both systems (and that's the substance of a different book), but for now, we'll simply keep it at this: America does not have a "leaving examinations" system.

Nevertheless, international students often transpose their conception of "leaving exams" onto the SAT and ACT. In other words, international students think that the SAT/ACT is the exam that Americans take at the end of their secondary school experience to cap off their studies and act as the basis of entry into US colleges.

Not the case. All students, regardless of country of origin and education system, must prepare independently of their normal school work to prepare for the SAT/ACT. And, yes, while some secondary schools do provide access to support, generally, it's a completely separate requirement. In this respect, all students are in the same boat.

MYTH 2:
Schools are easier on international students

Schools do consider the circumstances of international students, but in truth, applying as an international student is just as difficult, if not more so, than applying as an American.

Some students think that since they are "coming from a foreign country," schools will be less selective in their admissions choices and assess them based on different score ranges. This may in fact be true, but it really depends on where you're coming from. My mentors in admissions taught me that schools want to create "a microcosm of the world" on campus, and to do so admissions directors seek a diverse class from as many different countries as possible—but they also want talent.

So, yes, a student who defects from Cuba, washes up on the shores of Miami, walks into a testing center and scores in the 85th percentile is pretty special. However, if you're coming from a world center like London, Shanghai, Singapore, or the such, where access to good support exists and the historical application standards are high, it's a wholly different story. The application pools from those markets are as competitive as any in the world.

So while, in some cases, colleges can display flexibility in admissions based a student's country of origin and background, the standards are as competitive as they are in places like New York, Chicago, or Silicon Valley. And that's good—it inspires you to work hard, commit yourself to improving, and brings out your best, all of which translates to your best scores.

MYTH 3:
You have it harder than anybody else

Another question I hear often from test-takers: "Don't they understand that I'm in the middle of [A-Levels]?"

Yes, they do. They also understand that other students around the world are taking the IB, that Americans are taking Advanced Placement exams and school finals, that the Chinese are taking Gao Kao, that the French are sitting the French Bac, and that students across Africa are taking multiple terminal exams in multiple countries on multiple timelines. In short, everybody is in the same boat. It's long been that way, and it will likely continue. Embrace it. Love it.

Another common refrain is a concern that standardized tests favor American students. When the Redesigned SAT debuted a few years back, the exam profile mentioned that the Evidence-Based Reading section would feature "Great Texts of Western Literature." Many international students (and particularly those outside of the UK) felt at a disadvantage, worried that they could not compete with American students, especially on American-based texts. Well, I have news for you: American students don't know them either!

REALITY 1:
You know more than we do

Many international students do not understand that they possess a number of distinct advantages over American students. While Americans study a broader range of subjects over their time in high school, most other systems study their subjects more deeply. As a result, you know more about what you know than we know about what we know.

This point comes into focus on SAT Subject Tests, in particular. Whereas most US students know a nice deal about almost all of the information on the exam, international students know at least one or two more layers of depth on the topics that they have in common with US students. This is a good thing for international students, as it means that their total amount of work required to prepare for the SAT Subject Tests is less than that of an American student. This is a chief reason, especially in Math and Science, that international students do so well on SAT Subject Tests.

REALITY 2:
You know less than we do

Balancing the point above, however, students coming from an American system do, in fact, study a broader range of topics in a particular subject. Thus, for American students, fewer concepts on the exam will be entirely unfamiliar; but, again, for the ones that American and non-American students have in common, the non-American students almost always know them better.

To illustrate, on the SAT Physics Subject Test, a typical American student will recognize 90% of the material by the time May comes around, whereas an international student will recognize closer to 80%. However, on a given diagnostic test at that time, an American student may score a 670 whereas the international student would earn a 720.

Best Practices for Institutions

CATES has run successful institutional programs in partnership with schools and charities across the globe. Below, you can find some tips and advice on how to replicate our success at your own institution.

- **Student accountability:** students must be made accountable to attend test preparation sessions. If all sessions are not required, students may lose incentive to attend—especially if they have not paid for the class. As a result, students' scores suffer.
- **Family support:** families must be on-board with the program. Fostering a symbiotic relationship with the student's family is a win-win for everyone involved. The class leaders and the families can reinforce any insight or wisdom provided by the other party in helping students prepare for testing and admission. By hearing consistent encouragement in different contexts, students can develop the comfort and confidence to succeed more easily.

- **Class size:** keep groups small. Once the number of students extends beyond four or five, the dynamic in the room changes. While classes of ten or more can be successful, small groups help keep sessions focused, on-track, and wholly productive.
- **Cluster properly:** endeavor to match students with similar needs so that sessions can be targeted in their focus. Clusters can be based on CATES's analysis of previous testing and/or mock test results.
- **Individualized instruction:** simply, find a way to make it happen. Class leaders must find time to sit with each student individually, either over the course of the program or during a private session. There is no substitute for private prep and it's a real difference maker.
- **Mock tests:** an essential component of the test preparation process. Students must take advantage of free mock tests: a direct relationship exists between the number of mock tests a student takes and their ultimate score.
- **Open score-sharing policy:** particularly in small groups (two to five students), students should feel comfortable discussing their results in order to measure performance in relation to their diagnostic and target scores.

About

Who We Are

Founded in 2002 by Chris Ajemian, CATES offers support with education planning, academics, test prep, applications, and careers. An unwavering personal focus and individually-tailored methodology inform everything we do, whether it's private tutoring and classes or online and institutional programs. Our goal is simple: to provide the tools and resources you need to transform your life.

Since 2002, we have worked closely with families and schools in the US, UK, and Europe to design and support personalized education programs that maximize students' potential by focusing holistically on the academic, psychological, emotional, and physical elements of learning. Working with CATES to achieve their goals gives students an opportunity to acquire new skills, develop new learning habits, and build a confidence in their own abilities that will carry them far beyond any class, test, or application, and into the next phase of their lives.

Methodology

We believe that methodology matters. CATES programs combine cutting-edge educational techniques, AI-powered performance analysis, and individually customized tools to achieve superior learning outcomes. Our personal, learner-centered approach analyzes both the cognitive and affective factors behind performance, helping students to develop the 'soft skills' and personal qualities required for success in education and beyond. Guided by our expert tutors, students build the confidence, dedication, and passion needed to excel both now and later in life.

Program Design Principles

All of our programs adhere to three key principles:

- From intake to graduation, the process is entirely learner-centered and mastery-based.
- Program components are integrated contextually to facilitate responsive, individualized instruction.
- High-quality resources and tools are sourced or created according to each student's evolving needs.

Big-Picture Thinking, Long-Term Planning

Programs are tailored to integrate within a coherent scheme for the learner's broader educational and professional goals. Utilizing proven motivational techniques and rich longitudinal data, our focus on big-picture thinking motivates students to capitalize on their intrinsic talents today to foster success tomorrow.

Organization

Education and organization go hand in hand. Using the CATES Core, our competency-based curriculum, CATES students benefit from a structured learning plan that incorporates best-in-class insight for students at each stage of the learning journey.

Dynamic Leadership

CATES leadership works directly with learners and is actively involved in developing innovative pedagogical techniques to further student success. Continuing professional development ensures that we stay current with developments in education—both in academia and the marketplace—to create superior tools for lasting learning.

Blended Learning

No two students are the same, and neither are two CATES programs. We utilize a multi-faceted tool kit, including textbooks, downloadable software, mobile apps, and online tools to provide a rich educational experience within a contemporary education model customized to each student's needs and learning style.

Our Model

1. Assessment

All CATES programs begin with an assessment. We may ask to review a recent school test, for students to sit a diagnostic mock test, or for students to send their resume to establish a baseline for dialogue.

2. Analysis

Whatever the assessment, our in-house experts perform a comprehensive analysis of the results and generate a report that identifies possible cognitive and affective factors at play. These questions lead our initial conversations with the student to help confirm strengths and needs.

3. Strategy

Once we confirm the circumstances, our team designs an individualized program to power student success, leveraging the student's talents to launch from a position of strength and confidence.

4. Support

Our experts guide the initial steps in preparation for the student to, at some point, take the reins and lead the process. We remain involved every step of the way to provide guidance, context, and insight as the student grows and needs evolve.

5. Success

Success is a journey, not a destination. Whether the journey lasts two days, two months, or two years, CATES students experience accomplishment every step of the way and our experts reinforce student achievement to the end of the program—and beyond.

CATES Core

The CATES Core is our own proprietary problem-solving methodology, which focuses on the scholastic, psychological, and cultural aspects of the learning process. The Core is designed to teach students the content, strategies, and skills needed to realize their goals within their budget, scheduling needs, and time horizon, allowing them to succeed both in and outside the classroom and maximize outcomes. Student progress is tracked over time by our proprietary software, CATES HQ, an AI tool which assesses student exam performance and calculates an achievable target score and priorities for preparation.

These insights, alongside your tutor's qualitative analysis of your performance, guide further refinements of your learning plan to maximize your scoring potential.

Our disruptive and innovative approach to data underpins the success of this system. When looking at a student's diagnostic and mock test scores, we ask ourselves the following question: what forces led to the student's mistakes? It seems simple, yet the failure to insightfully answer this question is what causes students, whether working alone or with other prep companies, to see limited improvement in their scores. Our data points to strengths and weaknesses in specific academic domains and thus prioritizes what students must learn. It also suggests specific affective factors impacting the testing experience, thereby helping our tutors identify how best to frame ideas and concepts for individual students.

Years of applying our proprietary system to student improvement has provided us with some generalizable insights into how students respond to the testing experience—and, more specifically, why they make the mistakes they do. Students often answer questions incorrectly for the following reasons:

- Need to learn the content
- Need to learn test-specific strategy
- Need to test with more focus and/or care

Perhaps more important than these broad categories, however, are the individual forces that underpin students' mistakes. These may include:

- Gaps between school subject curriculum and material tested on exam
- Recent or historical lack of testing confidence
- Need to better apply strategies specific to the test
- Need to develop management of thought and emotion during the testing experience
- Undiagnosed learning difference
- Extenuating circumstances of testing environment
- X-Factors

These forces all influence the student's mindset during the test-taking experience and directly impact the score.

Once this "real data" has been identified and organized, the student can develop a better sense of what score they can expect on test day. While every test will present something new, if the student can eliminate (ideally) all their controllable mistakes, the student can set accurate target scores and plan prep accordingly. With reasonable target scores backed up by an achievable plan, the student feels empowered to approach the process with confidence.

Institutional Programs

CATES partners with schools, businesses, and organizations to design comprehensive on-site programs that help students improve their standardized test scores, graduate with strong grades, and earn acceptance to top-tier secondary schools and colleges. From conceptualization to evaluation, we collaborate with your educational leaders to build and refine our programs through an iterative process of development, adapting our proprietary learning tools and strategies to best meet your students' needs.

Our Institutional team has designed programs for CTP-4, ISEE/SSAT, SAT, Subject Tests, ACT, TOEFL, IB, and application preparation. Our scalable methodology has proven successful across class sizes from three to 300 and program durations from 1 afternoon to 78 weeks. CATES programs foster a collaborative and project-based learning environment in which students engage via in-class instruction and online class communities to achieve their educational goals.

CATES programs are designed to promote a culture of self-motivated internal exploration, in addition to academic success. Aiming to maximize the potential of each individual student with respect to their ability, we focus on building emotional confidence and strategic-thinking skills from program outset.

We have run institutional programs in partnership with schools and charities all over the world, including Poly Prep (NYC), Chess-in-the-Schools, City of London School, Dun & Bradstreet, International School of Brussels, and Yale Young African Scholars, among others. CATES also runs the most successful US preparation program in Europe—the Sutton Trust US Program—in collaboration with the US-UK Fulbright Commission, Harvard, Yale, and MIT. Our institutional programs have helped students gain access to top schools, such as Harvard, Yale, Princeton, MIT, and Stanford, as well as millions of dollars in financial aid.

Institutional Partners also benefit from our Teacher Advantage Program—after partnering with CATES, all staff at your school or non-profit will be eligible for discounted rates on CATES services.

Team

CATES's success is founded on its people. We seek exceptional tutors and staff to join our team, and we retain them by supporting their development into world-class professionals. CATES tutors excel not only in their subject area but also in effective communication and relationship-building. We hire people who recognize the nuances of individual learning styles and personalities and who can leverage this insight to build tailored educational strategies that maximize student outcomes. We also partner with like-minded organizations to provide seamless, high-quality education support in areas outside of our core competencies.

Head Tutor Team

The CATES Head Tutor Team leads the hiring and development of the CATES staff. The HTT trains all CATES tutors and makes sure that they stay current with the latest trends in standardized test preparation through regular master classes and advanced training seminars. Graduates of New York University, Stony Brook, Yale University, New York University, and Stanford, members of the HTT have each worked with middle school, high school, and graduate school students on test prep for over a decade.

Senior Associate Tutoring Staff

CATES Senior Associates are graduates of the top universities in the US, including Yale, Princeton, Harvard, Stanford, MIT,

University of Chicago, Columbia University, Brown, Dartmouth, and University of Pennsylvania, among others. The Senior Associates possess anywhere between 4 and 10 years of tutoring and test prep experience, and specialize in everything from ISEE to SAT to GMAT prep.

Associate Tutoring Staff

Associate Tutors possess at least three years of test prep experience in New York and are the life-blood of our company. Each CATES Associate is an energetic, dynamic, and engaging instructor who has graduated from a top-tier US college. Associate Tutors lead classes, work online with students overseas, and work privately with students one-on-one. The Associate Tutors bring new ideas to the table and allow CATES to stay current with the latest innovations in test prep and fresh on the ever-changing tastes and interests of our students.

Contact Information

For more information, please visit our website at https://catestutoring.com.

To get in touch, choose the best point of contact from the list below. We look forward to hearing from you!

General Inquiries:

info@catestutoring.com
US: +1 (212) 359-4208
UK: +44 (0)20 3865 0654

Author:
Chris Ajemian, CATES Founder & CEO

The founder and CEO of CATES Tutoring & Education Services, Chris Ajemian is one of the world's foremost authorities on standardized test preparation. Together with his team at CATES, Chris has transformed the lives of thousands of families across the United States and as far abroad as Africa, India, and China. Students working with Chris and CATES have improved their SAT scores by more than 400 points and their ACT scores by more than 10, earning them admission to Top 25 universities and over $60M in financial aid. Chris has been recognized by the Obie Award-winning Chocolate Factory Theater in NYC with its inaugural Artist in Industry Award for his creative contributions to the education field and is a featured expert in The Test & The Art of Thinking, a groundbreaking documentary that explores the role of standardized testing in American culture.

Chris holds a Bachelor of Arts in Pre-Med and Theater Arts from Boston College, where he won the J. Paul Marcoux Award for Academic & Artistic Excellence, and he completed his Specialization in Entrepreneurship through the Wharton School of Business. He also holds the distinction of being the first-ever enrollee in the Special Students in Education program for professional educators at the Harvard Graduate School of Education, where he will finish his master's in Technology, Innovation, and Education in 2019.

www.ingramcontent.com/pod-product-compliance
Lightning Source LLC
Chambersburg PA
CBHW061220070526
44584CB00029B/3918